THE DUMBEST GUY AT THE TABLE

T0342890

UPDATED EDITION

THE DUMBEST GUY AT THE TABLE

DAVID SHEIN

echo

PUBLISHING

An imprint of Bonnier Books UK
Level 45, World Square,
680 George Street
Sydney NSW 2000
www.echopublishing.com.au

Bonnier Books UK
4th Floor, Victoria House,
Bloomsbury Square
London WC1B 4DA
www.bonnierbooks.co.uk

Echo Publishing acknowledges the traditional custodians of Country throughout Australia. We recognise their continuing connection to land, sea and waters. We pay our respects to Elders past and present.

First published 2022

This edition published 2023

Printed and bound in Australia by Griffin Press

The paper this book is printed on is certified against the Forest Stewardship Council® Standards. Griffin Press holds chain of custody certification SGSHK-COC-005088. FSC® promotes environmentally responsible, socially beneficial and economically viable management of the world's forests.

Cover design: Design by Committee

Page design and layout: transformer.com.au

Pages 94–97: 'The First XV: 15 All Black Principles' is summarised from James Kerr, *Legacy: What the All Blacks can teach us about business and life*, Little, Brown Book Group, London 2015

A catalogue entry for this book is available from the National Library of Australia

ISBN: 9781760688370 (paperback)
ISBN: 9781760687441 (ebook)

echo_publishing

echo_publishing

echopublishingaustralia

Dedication

This book is dedicated to my good friend and work colleague Dan Jarzin, who tragically passed away, much too young, on 10 August 2005.

To everyone, Dan was this good-looking, world-class financial controller, an amazing Iron Man triathlete with a beautiful wife, Mary, and two adorable kids – he had everything. Unfortunately, Dan did not see what everyone else did, and he succumbed to his illness. In memory of Dan, 100 per cent of the royalties received by the author on book sales will be donated to the Black Dog Institute, www.blackdoginstitute.org.au.

Dan was the third person to join Com Tech, although he left after six months to join a more established company. He returned as our CFO and made a massive contribution to Com Tech. Dan, you always told me to write a book – it took me more than 20 years, but finally I have taken your advice.

About the author

In June 1987, David Shein – having recently migrated to Australia from South Africa – founded Com Tech Communications as a specialist supplier of networking and communications products. Fourteen years later, he sold the business to Dimension Data at an enterprise value of over $1 billion. At the time of sale, Com Tech employed over 1400 people, with offices Australia-wide and revenues of $700 million. The business was profitable from inception, never used any external debt, and was regularly voted as one of the leading companies to work for in Australia.

Since then, David has been actively involved in mentoring young management teams and investing in a number of startups, many of which have been successfully exited. He serves as an investor and board member for some innovative Australian startups, which include cyber-security company Kasada; Advanced Navigation, a leader in positioning solutions from the seabed to a satellite; and Simpology, a fintech company providing disruptive home-loan origination software. David is co-founder of OIF VC, an early-stage venture capital fund that invests in interesting Australian startups, as well as a founding partner in Israeli venture capital enterprise OurCrowd, the first global equity-based crowd-funding platform.

Foreword

by Ian Chappell

David Shein wasn't always the dumbest guy at the table; I attended a lot of board meetings he convened.

I first met David in 1966 when I was invited to the Shein home in Johannesburg by his father, Martin. The first in a family full of accountants, Martin was head of the Dugson clothing company in Johannesburg, which generously supplied the touring Australian cricket team with blazers and other assorted apparel.

Little did I know that when I allowed myself to be bowled by this six-year-old South African kid in a pick-up game in his father's backyard it would be one of my lucky breaks in life. I couldn't help adding 'allowed myself to be bowled', because for too long David Shein has laboured under the misapprehension that he genuinely beat my forward defensive shot.

This was in 1966. If David had bowled me in his father's backyard in 1970 then it would've been a genuine dismissal. My second tour of South Africa was so calamitous that I would have been eager to score runs even in a Whiteley Road backyard.

Meeting Martin in 1966 began a long and happy relationship with the Shein family that has endured until the present.

Our families have a lot in common. They both consist of three boys, an influential mother and a strong-willed father named Martin. When the two fathers met at The Oval in London in 1972, it was the first occasion that brothers – Greg and myself – made centuries on the same day of a Test. To celebrate, father Shein said to father Chappell: 'I'll send you a suit via one of the boys when they visit South Africa at the end of the tour.'

True to his word, I carried home a suit for Dad that fitted him perfectly, judged purely on that face-to-face meeting at The Oval.

That tells you two things about the male Sheins: they are men of their word and they have a sharp eye for detail.

Those qualities were evident in the way Com Tech and then later DiData was run.

When the boys started arriving in Sydney in the 1980s, my wife Barbara-Ann and I often caught up with them socially. Once David started Com Tech in 1987 I gradually became involved with the business, occasionally addressing the staff, helping to organise current and ex-cricketers to play in their client golf days and eventually serving on the board.

Apart from enjoying myself immensely, I learnt a lot about business and the way David conducted operations. He, along with brothers Jon and Steven, ran a highly successful business by applying some very simple rules.

I'd always been of the strong belief that the same principles that apply to running a successful sporting team also work well in both business and life.

Applying common sense is an important part of any successful venture, and David has always valued that ingredient.

Reading through his book, the things that stand out about his business life are all lessons I learnt during my cricket career.

For example you always learn more from your losses than your wins. As a leader it pays to empower the people under you – because, in the case of a cricket team, eleven heads are better than one. Winning at any cost is not a victory, but succeeding while maintaining integrity ensures long-term fulfilment.

I always advised young cricketers to choose the bat they liked, not the one that paid the highest royalties. It generally follows that if you perform well, the money takes care of itself.

As a captain I had a saying about the way you treat players: 'Praise in public and castigate in private.'

David's thoughtful treatment of staff is legendary, and that is why he still maintains contact with a number of the people who worked under him during both the Com Tech and DiData period. He also applied a similar approach with clients, and I have no doubt it was a trait that sealed many important partnerships, particularly in those crucial early days of Com Tech.

He's also believed in a balance between mixing business with relaxation. There was no better example of this than the famous forums that were held at Hyatt Coolum. The idea of having the IT industry gather under one roof and deliver presentations on products old and new, was one of pure genius. However, the sun going down wasn't the end of proceedings and the entertainment that followed was of a similar high quality to the presentations delivered during the day.

To listen to the wonderful singing voice of Kate Ceberano or be amused by the humour of Danny McMaster was an absolute pleasure. Nevertheless, my favourite act was the truly amazing Chinese gymnasts who were masterfully introduced with the succinct statement: 'These guys do some really sick shit.'

The performers who followed were brilliant and fully lived up to the introduction.

As a businessman, David Shein has lived up to his ideals. Don't be fooled by the title of this book; this guy really knows his shit.

Ian Chappell
Australian Cricket Captain, 1971–1975

Contents

Preface

by David Shein

Two decades after selling the company that I founded, Com Tech Communications, for an enterprise value of over $1 billion – arguably Australia's first tech unicorn – I decided to write a book.

Hopefully the lessons provided in this book will provide valuable advice to anyone looking to start a company or to anyone who is managing a team of people. One of the benefits of turning 60 back in 2020 is that I have been around long enough to see products come and go. But what hasn't changed is that every company still has staff, customers and business partners. I firmly believe that the way you treat these three constituents will determine whether you build a good company, a great company, an irrelevant company or one that simply disappears.

While achieving financial success has been a great outcome for myself and my family, there are so many other fulfilling outcomes of building a successful company. Seeing people, including myself, achieve way more professionally than they ever thought possible; seeing staff members who helped to build the company share in the success of the company; and, importantly, that feeling of being part of a phenomenal team that achieved something great – we would all have done anything for each other.

One of the two greatest compliments that I received after selling Com Tech came from Bob Dwyer, Australian Rugby World Cup winning coach and Com Tech board member, who said: 'Dave, you taught me that you don't have to be an asshole to build a successful company.' The other came from my best friend and founder of Nando's (the world's best chicken), Robbie Brozin, who told me: 'Dave, you're still the same guy that you were when you left South Africa in 1986 – you haven't changed.'

While I achieved more than I ever dreamed I was capable of, it pales into insignificance when you compare it with the success of the next generation of founders – companies like SEEK, carsales.com, REA and WiseTech Global. But then, the third generation of founders have truly shown what this country is capable of delivering to the world. Scott and Mike from Atlassian, Mel and Cliff from Canva, Larry and Pete from Zip, Nick and Anthony from Afterpay and all the rest have proven that Australia has emerged as an innovation powerhouse.

I should explain right at the outset that the Com Tech sales model was a traditional business-to-business sales model. This sales-led growth was driven by account executives who built relationships with the buyer, usually the CTO, who generally purchased the industry-standard market-leading product from a partner who he/she believed would deliver the best service and support at a fair price. The advent of the cloud has provided alternative sales methods, including marketing-led growth, where marketing targeted business execs who made purchasing decisions on KPIs (key performance indicators) and ROI (return on investment). And the latest sales model is the end-user era, where product-led growth drives sales – Atlassian was the pioneer and famously built Australia's most successful tech company without hiring a salesperson. All three methods still have their place, and in OIF VC's own portfolio each company has chosen their individual method for driving sales. What I do know is that no matter the method, NOTHING HAPPENS UNTIL YOU SELL SOMETHING.

I truly believe that Australia is the Scale-Up Nation. I am convinced that the next generation of founders will provide even more success for our great nation, and together with my partners at OIF I am so proud to be a small part of the innovation ecosystem, trying to uncover the next big thing! There has never been a better time to be Australian.

● ● ●

Introduction

I always say that I could write a book on lucky breaks – and the book would be bloody thick.

So many things have happened in my life that if even one decision had gone a different way, I probably would not be writing now. Hopefully, once you've read it, *you'll* feel lucky that I had so many breaks. As Eleanor Roosevelt said: 'Learn from the mistakes of others. You can't live long enough to make them all yourself.'

One of the luckiest was emigrating to Australia in 1986, with a young wife, Colleen, and an eight-month-old baby, Jarred. This clearly is the lucky country.

I arrived in Australia on Saturday 8 November and started work on Monday 10 November. Having left Price Waterhouse (which wasn't yet PwC) as a junior clerk, when I got a job in a new country as national sales manager of a distribution company selling business software, I thought I had hit the jackpot. Boy, did I learn so much. In life and business, you don't just learn lessons from how *well* people do things. Sometimes you can learn even more by observing how *not* to do things. It was probably the latter case that led me to start my own company nine months later – in that first job in Australia, I was paid badly, had no job satisfaction and wasn't allowed any input into how the company should be run. That turned out to be the luckiest break of my life. If I'd loved my job and been paid a market-related salary, I would never, ever have started my own company. In fact, my mother-in-law told me to 'get a job like any normal South African' and not take the unnecessary risk of founding my own company when I was a new migrant with a wife and young son. Mind you, two years later she did say, 'Why didn't you give me any shares!?'

At the distribution company, I was on a salary of $2000 a month. One of my customers, Gary Buttsworth from Logical Solutions, offered me a job for $4000. I told Gary that I had always wanted to try something on my own and that if things didn't work out after six months, I wouldn't be too proud to come back to see him – and hopefully he wouldn't be too proud to give me the job. Luckily, I never needed to go back, but I always valued the confidence and time that Gary gave me. My opportunity cost was so low, I knew that I only had to earn $2000 a month just to be where I already was. If I was ever going to become a founder, this was my opportunity.

I established Com Tech Communications in June 1987, as a one-man band distributing networking products to computer resellers. PCs were already becoming pervasive in the work environment, but it was only in about 1987 that local area networks started being installed in corporations.

I learnt from my first job in Australia that if I had left because of those three factors around poor salary, low job satisfaction and having no input, then anybody I might hire would probably feel the same if they found themselves in a similar situation. I was only 26 when I started my company and had never run a business or hired anyone in my life – maybe that was a lucky break too. Being young and naïve, I was fearless. I just ran Com Tech on common sense. But, as someone once told me, the problem with common sense is that it's not too common. So, don't expect to find rocket science in this book. I always say that if you put me at any table, I can guarantee that I will have the lowest IQ of anyone sitting there – and so I wrote this book: *The Dumbest Guy at the Table*. I often work with companies that are developing groundbreaking technology, but they just don't get the basics of company culture right – they overcomplicate things. Simplicity is the ultimate sophistication.

Since 1987, I have hired hundreds of outstanding people, knowing that if I paid well, listened to their valuable ideas and ensured that they loved coming to work every day, I could still be part of something great, even if I was the dumbest guy at the table.

These principles have formed the basis of my management style for 35 years, and hopefully will continue to do so for many more years to come. It's these same principles that I have applied to building our venture capital fund, OIF – after all, how can we add value to our portfolio companies without an exceptional team of people?

With experience, I have learnt that products come and go. But you will always have customers, staff and business partners. How you treat these three constituents will be the difference between building a good company, a great company, an irrelevant company or one that simply disappears. This is exactly why I have chosen to write a book two decades after I sold Com Tech. So much has changed – yet, in some ways, nothing has changed.

In sharing the experience I have gained over the past 35 years, I hope that I am able to add some value to what you do.

That's why I get out of bed every day – I want to make a difference.

● ● ●

In life and business you don't just learn lessons from how *well* people do things. Sometimes you learn even more by observing how *not* to do things.

CHAPTER 1

So, you wanna be a founder?

My father, Martin, told me that it would be better to earn 50 cents for yourself than $1 from someone else.

That advice is exactly the opposite of what I would tell any of my three boys.

Why would you want the aggravation, challenges and heartache of running your own business, when you could earn twice as much in a job without the stress? What's more, I've seen people make lots of money working at multinationals like Amazon, Microsoft and Apple, and closer to home Macquarie Bank, Atlassian, Afterpay, Zip, WiseTech Global and

Canva – to name just a few – earning huge salaries and seeing their stock options soar in value.

However, if any of my three sons wanted to have a go, I would back them to the hilt. But I *would* say to them that:

- IF after a reasonable period of time, you're not earning at least as much as you would in a job, AND
- you're not building an asset that you can sell one day, THEN ...

DON'T WASTE YOUR BLOODY TIME!

Being a founder or a business manager is tough, make no mistake about it (see chapter 6). I remember when one of the team at Com Tech said, 'Dave, I'm worried, you look tired.' To which I replied, 'You should worry when I *don't* look tired.'

Com Tech was like another child – I lived and dreamed it 24/7. Every day I was thinking: *What can we be doing better for our staff and customers? What do we need to do to keep winning?* In a fast-changing world, with increased competition, reduced margins and customers demanding better customer service, you have to be thinking this every single day.

I remember when we had our first large bad debt. I was devastated. I called my dad in South Africa and told him that we had just written off $70,000 because a customer of ours (HiSoft Computers) had gone bankrupt. My dad asked how much business we had done with them over the years.

'$3 million,' I replied.

'And what was your profit margin?'

'30 per cent, Dad.'

'So you made $900,000 and lost $70,000 – not a bad deal.'

But what he said next still rings in my ears.

'My boy, if you chop wood, you get splinters.'

And how right he was. If you're going to be in business, you're going to have setbacks. If you do karate, you have to be willing to take the knocks – it goes with the territory.

I couldn't explain the skills required for a founder any better than Jack Welch, legendary CEO of General Electric. Jack suggested that you need the four 'E's of leadership to succeed.

1. Do you have the **ENERGY** to be a founder? There are so many challenges, both in and out of your control, that require so much energy. To give an example: as CEO, when you drew up your budget at the start of 2020, you didn't take into account that there would be a global pandemic shutting down large parts of the global economy. What impact will this have on your business, positive or negative, given you have already prepared your budget and didn't bank on this eventuality?

2. Do you have the ability to **ENERGISE** a team of people to be the best that they can possibly be? One of the most important traits that we look for in a founder is their ability to sell. Will they be able to win those early customers, and convince key people to leave a secure role because the founder has sold them on their vision? Great founders enable their team to achieve more than would have been possible in another environment. I can tell you that this is one of the most satisfying parts of being a founder. I have seen people, including myself, achieve goals they had never dreamed of attaining. When I started Com Tech I never would have believed that I was capable of running a national company with 1400 people – after all, I had never hired a single person prior to Com Tech. Miracles happen when you are part of a great team with a great culture.

3. Do you have the **EDGE** to make those tough Yes or No decisions? Should I fire my best salesperson because they do not share the values of the company? Should we open an office in the USA? Should we launch a new product ... or scrap a non-performing one? Do we need to pivot our business because our original business plan just hasn't stacked up

the way we expected? Sometimes people won't make a decision until they are 100 per cent sure of the facts. However, even *with* all the data and analysis, you will never be 100 per cent sure. There is always risk involved, and by the time you get to your 100 per cent, the opportunity will probably be gone. Never have founders been more tested than when the economy changed: inflation rose; interest rates rose; and cheap, easy capital became unbelievably tough to get. Founders who have the edge to deal with changed conditions will survive – those who don't will lose their dream.

4. Do you have the ability to **EXECUTE** on your business plan? Lots of startups and plans look terrific on a PowerPoint presentation and an Excel spreadsheet. Great founders have the ability to execute on the plan – or pivot when things don't go as expected.

When I ask founders why they want to start a company, some reply, 'I want to be a millionaire,' or 'I want to build a unicorn.' Most successful founders haven't had either of those ambitions as their number one goal; it generally happens as a consequence of building a great company. Ask Jeff Bezos, Bill Gates or Scott Farquhar. Entrepreneurs usually have a vision that goes way beyond money.

Consider Elon Musk – he sold PayPal to eBay and exited with $US160 million. Instead of going to chill on a beach, he chose to put $100 million into SpaceX and $60 million into Tesla – he bet the entire farm on building the next big thing, or in this case the next big things.

Here's another piece of advice to a founder. There's no issue when a sportsperson wants to win – it only becomes an issue when a sportsperson wants to win at all costs. Lance Armstrong wanting to win the Tour de France was not the problem – wanting to *win at all costs* became his problem. The same applies in business. Wanting to succeed is great, but succeeding at any cost is not an option. You can make money, lots of it, but you can't lose your reputation, not a shred of it. Running your business with integrity should always be top of mind.

● ● ●

Miracles happen when you are part of a great team with a great culture.

CHAPTER 2

The Power of Two – do I need a co-founder?

I always tell my boys that you can only make one bad decision in life, and that relates to who you marry.

Choose the right partner and any problem is surmountable. Choose the wrong partner and when the going gets tough (and even the best marriages face challenges – financial issues, illness, emigration, death of a loved one) they run for the hills.

To me, the best way to depict a good relationship is to take a triangle and draw a line down the middle: as long as the two triangles are balanced, relationships work. Never forget that one party is responsible for 50 per cent of any relationship and another party is responsible for the other 50 per cent. Have you ever had a friendship where you feel that you are doing everything for the relationship and they never do anything? Eventually something has got to give.

The same principle applies to your relationships with family, friends and at work. Both parties have to know what value they need to add to each other to keep those two triangles in balance. So, when you choose a co-founder, it's essential that you both know exactly what is expected of each of you to ensure that you keep adding value to each other. As your company grows, make sure that you keep re-evaluating how those obligations may change as the challenges of a growing business evolve.

Once, at a staff induction day, someone said to me, 'Dave, that's not true, I've just had a baby and all I do is change nappies and feed him.' I responded by saying, 'I have a dad who's nearly 80 and I'm pushing him around in a wheelchair.' When you look at a relationship, don't look at it on a day-to-day basis, look at it over a reasonable period of time – and make sure that you are contributing what's expected of you and that the other side of the triangle is delivering whatever is expected of them. So, whether you are a founder, a parent, a child, a friend, a spouse, an employer or employee, understand that you have certain expectations to meet. There is always another party involved who is relying

GOOD RELATIONSHIP

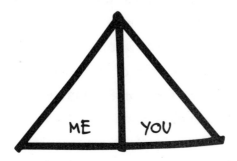

ME | YOU

BAD RELATIONSHIP

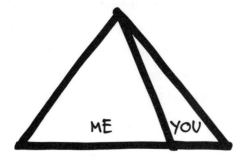

ME | YOU

on you to meet your side of the bargain. Make sure that you are aligned.

The same is true for a business partner. Business is tough, make no mistake about it. Even when it's going well, it's taxing. How do we fund our growth? How do we continue to attract and retain the same high-quality resources that we secured as a startup? How do we ensure that the level of service that we provide is consistent across regions? Running a company requires a tremendous amount of energy – you are constantly dealing with things that are in your control and things that are out of your control.

Choosing the right business partner can help alleviate the strain – that pillar of support will always be there when you most need it. Some of the world's greatest companies have been started by co-founders. I call it the Power of Two: the two Steves at Apple, Bill and Paul at Microsoft, Larry and Sergey at Google, and – closer to home – Mike and Scott from Atlassian, Nick and Anthony at Afterpay, Mel and Cliff from Canva, and Larry and Peter at Zip. In fact, we backed Larry and Peter because Larry was the front-of-house founder, while we saw such a safe and steady pair of hands in Peter, who would be looking after the back of house – a critical component of a business that was going to be lending money. Even looking back on my own career, while I may have been the sole founder, my brother Jon and I ran the company together – I used to worry about tomorrow while Jon worried about today.

The key to finding the right partner is simple, but fundamental. You not only need complementary skills, so that you are able to add value to one another, but, just as importantly, you also need to share like-minded values. I reckon in all the examples I have listed above, 1 + 1 = 3. But I'm sure that for every success, there are many more failures.

In a nutshell: when choosing a co-founder or a business partner, once you've made that call, it's very hard to get out of it. Make sure that you're not doing it because it's daunting to start a company on your own – it's a whole lot worse running a company when you're dealing with a misaligned partner. So, make sure that you each have complementary skills and a similar mindset and that you would be willing to go into battle with your partner when the shit hits the fan. And trust me, if it hasn't yet, it will. Ask Mark Zuckerberg, Bill Gates, Elon Musk or Larry and Pete at Zip.

● ● ●

CHAPTER 3

Rules for success

I often think about what contributed to my success.

When I define 'success', it's not necessarily just about having a great financial outcome. Of course, that is why you start a company, but success is a lot more than just the money. We sold Com Tech to a South African company, Dimension Data (so our company, having started out as Com Tech, finished up under the name Dimension Data), for an enterprise value of over $1 billion in 2000. Possibly Australia's first unicorn – but the word 'unicorn' was still only a beast with a single large horn back in those days.

Yep, we sold just before the dot-com crash. I told you I could write a book on lucky breaks.

Financial success is one of the reasons you take the risk to start your own company, but I'm just as proud that the company I sold in 2000 is still one of

Australia's leading integration companies. Several of the same management team who worked with me for many years are still in place. Some have been there for over 30 years. Boy, did we have a team. I'm proud that I still see people today who say that they have never had a better job than the one they had at Com Tech, and I'm proud that some of the world's largest companies – including Microsoft and Cisco – still remember the mutually beneficial partnership that we enjoyed. In a later chapter, I will talk about our culture: we lived and breathed customer and staff satisfaction, and we treated our business partners as an extension of our company. It paid off.

So, what do I consider to be the reasons for Com Tech's success?

Luck

Who would ever have thought that a skinny 12-year-old boy from Louisville, Kentucky, would become heavyweight champion of the world – and arguably one of the greatest human beings to set foot on this planet? When young Cassius Marcellus Clay Jr, later Muhammad Ali, realised that his bicycle had been stolen, he was furious and swore that he would 'whup' whoever stole it. When he went to report it, Joe Martin, a cop who ran the local gym, told Clay: 'You better learn how to box first.' Who could have imagined that a kid stealing Muhammad Ali's bicycle would be the lucky break that kickstarted the career of the greatest boxer of all time? Of course Muhammad Ali trained hard, but if his bike hadn't been stolen, would he have achieved the same success in another chosen career? Highly unlikely.

As I mentioned earlier, so many things have happened in my life that had any decision gone another way, I would not be writing this book. Everyone says that we worked hard. Of course we did. So did Jimmy at the corner cafe – he was at work before I left my house and was usually there when I came home. He was working hard, but he didn't have the same success that I did – because, unlike him, I happened to be in the right industry at the right time and, importantly, had lots of lucky breaks (not to mention the fact that Com Tech executed extremely well).

One of the luckiest breaks was being signed up as Novell's second distributor in Australia. Novell was the hottest company in the world at that time (1989). Novell country manager, Peter Stanford, had much easier options available than signing Com Tech. There were just three of us in the company, working out of a tiny terrace office at no. 72 Erskine Street, in Sydney's CBD. We were one of 27 companies applying for the distribution agreement and we were not the logical choice – there were large public companies in the mix, well funded, well staffed. But none had the hunger and passion that Com Tech had. The easy decision was Tech Pacific; the right decision was Com Tech.

We never let Novell down. We invested heavily in both people and infrastructure to ensure that we enhanced Novell's reputation in Australia. Peter said that if within 18 months we became as big as the original distributor, Datamatic, he would make no changes to the distribution channel. Within three months we were twice Datamatic's size. We were doing 70 per cent of Novell's business in Australia. Another lucky break was that Datamatic was so bad, we didn't even have to be good (except that we *were* good – unbelievably good) to win business. They had abused the privilege of being an exclusive distributor and had no regard for customer service. They were my best salespeople – they did so much selling for us and I didn't even have to pay them commission.

To my disappointment, six months after our appointment as the second distributor, Novell appointed two more distributors: Merisel, a giant US distributor, and Powerlan, a Melbourne-based distributor. Novell went from one exclusive partner to four distributors in six months. We never gave up any of our 70 per cent market share and the other three distributors shared the rest. Com Tech were lucky enough to have Datamatic as a competitor –

Powerlan and Merisel had Com Tech. All three of the other companies eventually went out of business because they did not have the critical mass to hold enough inventory or provide the infrastructure to support a highly technical product, as we could.

Critical mass is critical – excuse the pun – in any business. Peter left his job a year later, but *not* because he had appointed Com Tech – we never let Peter or Novell down, and I have no doubt that we enhanced their reputation in the region. Peter was replaced by an older, more conservative, country manager – Arthur Ehrlich. Arthur was a great guy from the USA, but no way would he have made the bold decision Peter took in signing up Com Tech as the second distributor. It would have been too risky, and he wouldn't have wanted to risk losing those valuable Novell stock options.

Hard work

I always say that it's easy to build a company, but unbelievably hard to build a great company. It's not what happens between 9 am and 5 pm that makes the difference, it's what you do before and after normal work hours. We invested heavily in relationships: staff, customers and business partners like Novell. We were forever out for breakfast, lunch and dinner, building those relationships and earning the trust of our key constituents. Meetings, seminars, conferences

– boy, that was hard. It didn't take long before I thought my wife was shrinking my jeans in the dryer. I put on about 15 kilos during my time as founder of Com Tech.

Focus

I always say that to succeed you need to be as focused as a one-eyed dog in a meat factory. Once we became the Novell distributor, the whole world wanted us to represent their products in Australia. We said no to 99 out of every 100 opportunities that we were offered.

When Steve Jobs took over at Apple, he cut their product range from 100 to 4. They became the first trillion-dollar company – not a bad outcome. And to further prove my point, I can give you $39 billion reasons why I am right. In seven years of operation, Afterpay initially had only one product – pay in four equal instalments. Whether you were in Sydney, New York or London, same simple product. I have no doubt that the service has improved, the interface, the integrations, the ability to drive customers to their merchants, but on the whole it's still buy now and pay later – the same product that revolutionised an industry. At the time of writing, Afterpay was only now ready to release its second product, Afterpay Money, to enable it to provide additional value to its very happy 3.5 million Australian customers. Focus on the significant few, not the insignificant many.

Team

You cannot build a great company on your own. I may not be the smartest person in the room, but I'm very confident at bringing the smartest people together. I employ people who are much smarter than me – but I'm not threatened by them. You have to surround yourself with an amazing, like-minded team who have not only the ability, but just as importantly the attitude, to differentiate your company from the competition.

At OIF Venture Capital, we see money as a commodity. There are a hundred other VCs to get your capital from – the only way we can differentiate ourselves is with the people who are adding value to our founders, who we see as our customers. Hopefully, by backing the right founders, together with the value that we can bring in addition to a cheque, we will deliver great outcomes for our other customers: our LPs (investors), who have entrusted *us* with their capital when they had other choices.

Later in the book, I dedicate a whole chapter to the importance of the team.

● ● ●

CHAPTER 4

Culture isn't important – it's *everything*

I truly believe that culture is the operating system of your company.

Every company has a culture. I'm not suggesting that what has worked for me over the years will work for everyone, but I couldn't manage a company any other way.

At Com Tech we simply said:

We GENUINELY take care of our

- customers
- staff
- business partners
- **shareholders**

Otherwise SOMEONE ELSE WILL.

You will notice that I have emphasised one of these important constituents: shareholders. Of course they're important, especially if you're one of them.

However, I sincerely believe that if you genuinely take care of customers, staff and business partners, then your shareholders are going to be well taken care of too.

Taking care of customers, staff and business partners would be so simple to achieve if you didn't have these other balls to juggle called cash flow and profitability. It would be easy to keep staff happy if you paid twice market-related salaries and told them, 'Hey, this is a stressful industry, so don't take four weeks leave, take eight.' As a staff member you would have to keep your CV current, because it wouldn't be too long before the company went broke and you needed to find a new job.

A buy now pay later (BNPL) provider offering a retailer its service for free when the industry average was a 4 per cent fee, or offering a full-featured product as a freemium version forever, would make you a great supplier – but for a very short period of time.

Somehow, you have to deliver unbelievably high levels of staff satisfaction, provide an amazing product combined with legendary customer service, and still make a buck at the same time. I told you this wasn't going to be easy.

I know that Com Tech's company philosophy was very similar to that of most companies. Did you ever hear a founder say: 'Our number one asset is our furniture; number two, motor vehicles; number three, computer equipment; and number four ... drum roll ... our staff'? Or: 'We don't give a shit about customer service'? Of course, every company says that 'Our number one asset is our staff and we are committed to providing legendary service' – but how many actually deliver?

The difference was, we really did! We walked the talk and that is what culture is all about. It's not about practising yoga at work, having a ping pong table in the lunch room or bringing your puppy to the office – it's doing what you say you're going to do, every single day. Whatever that may be.

Every day I worried about what more we could be doing for our customers and staff. I fully support Richard Branson's sentiment: 'Clients do not come first. Employees come first. If you take care of your employees, they will take care of the clients.' It's not rocket science – happy staff will lead to legendary customer service. Excellent customer service means higher sales, repeat business and referrals – there is no better salesperson than a happy customer.

You only realise the importance of culture when you work in a toxic environment. I was asked to chair a financial services company, which was built on aggregating a number of independent financial-planning companies. The aim was to combine a number of leading financial planners and then IPO the company (initial public offering – list the company on the ASX). The planners were going to make millions. The trouble was, nobody planned on a global financial crisis. The IPO was put on hold and the planners then thought: *What have we done?* They did it for money, not love, and when the cash disappeared, the shit hit the fan. Nobody wanted to be there, but it was too late.

At the time, the company was owned by a large private equity (PE) company and I agreed to help out to try and save the business. I committed 20 hours a week. I started work on a Monday and by lunchtime Tuesday I had done my 20 hours. I called the head of the PE firm and said, 'Bill, if I wanted to work this hard, I would be doing this for myself.' I needed help. He sent his board representative, Ben, to work with me. Ben is a seriously smart Harvard MBA – and someone I very much enjoyed working with. We really had complementary skills.

What surprised me most – and I will never forget this – was when Ben said to me, 'Dave, I never knew how important culture was until I met you.' That was a huge compliment, coming from someone like Ben. It was a good lesson for me, too. I wanted to see whether my management principles would be as effective in financial services as they had been in technology. They sure were – people are people. There is no difference between a financial planner and a Java developer.

There is no difference between a client looking for outstanding financial advice and a client looking for outstanding technical help. How much is culture worth? In this case, $160 million – that is what the PE firm eventually sold the company for. I know that it was pretty much zero when I got there.

But it could have been a whole lot worse. Ask Travis Kalanick, founder of Uber. Uber was supposed to IPO at $120 billion, but only got away at $75 billion – a $45 billion hole caused by a toxic culture. Instead of being able to focus solely on the business, the new Uber CEO Dara Khosrowshahi first had to fix Uber's culture. He's doing a great job!

As a founder, make sure that what you say, you do. My biggest fear as CEO was saying something and our staff or customers thinking 'What a load of crap.' Your words have to match your actions. As you grow, it is important to ensure that the management team you have hired not only meet their objectives, but also share the values of the company you've created. It's hard enough running a well-managed company – don't make it even harder by having a poor culture.

So, does a great culture mean a great business? You can't have a great business without a great strategy – but try executing a great strategy with a lousy culture. It just won't work.

● ● ●

Five key performance indicators for a successful company

In every company I've been involved with, I always recommend that each year the management team should do an honest assessment of how they've been executing against their plan.

I use the five key performance indicators (KPIs) listed on the next page, all of which are of equal importance – they don't belong in any particular order. If you get this right – and it's not easy – you will be on track to building a long-term, sustainable company.

You can use these KPIs to rate your company out of five, according to how you have performed over the past year. As founder, your job is to ensure that you achieve a higher rating this year in every one of the five categories, compared with your assessment of the business last year. Anything else and you're going backwards.

So, here are the five KPIs:

- Brand awareness
- Innovative performance
- Digital transformation/Productivity
- Profitability
- Cash flow

Brand awareness

Never in business history has it been as easy to build or destroy a brand as it is today. Consider how long it took Coca Cola or McDonald's to build a global brand, compared with Amazon, Google or Facebook. Afterpay became a household name in Australia after only a few years of operation. When you execute well, social media gives you the ability to build your brand at breakneck speed. But screw up, and all the good is gone.

Brand awareness is your ability to attract AND retain customers, staff and business partners to your company. There is nothing better than people knocking on your door saying, 'I want to work for you.' Bear in mind that headhunters, like your company, also have to meet sales targets to make their budget. My experience is that most want to place people to make their numbers, not because they have found the perfect new staff member for your company. At Com Tech, I don't think we used a recruiter for the first five years of our existence. All our staff came through referrals from our existing staff. And because we were a brand that people in the industry wanted to work for, we had the pick of the bunch. The quality was exceptional and the cost was zilch! Would you rather be the HR manager at Apple or Nokia?

Having industry-standard, market-leading business partners wanting your company to represent their products makes it a whole lot easier than begging 'me too' players to partner with you. Once Com Tech had secured Novell as our key business partner and did an exceptional job representing them, the whole world of networking and communications wanted us to be their partner in Australia. That's how we got SynOptics (now irrelevant) and then became Cisco's first global, two-tier distribution partner. You wouldn't have to be a great salesperson to get Harvey Norman to stock your products if you worked for Apple. That sale was made because of the unbelievable brand awareness that Apple has created globally. It would be a whole lot tougher if you worked for Blackberry.

Customers

In every company that I have been involved with, customer service generally wins the day. Repeat customers keep coming back and are willing to try new products and services from your company. Remember, Amazon started out selling books. Uber started with hire cars. All great leaders, like Jeff Bezos, commit their company to what Bezos calls 'fanatical' customer service. How often have you bought a product or used a service because a friend or associate recommended it? A happy customer is the best salesperson that a company can have, and all it costs is delivering legendary customer service to your existing customers – not a dollar spent on marketing. With social media so pervasive, companies live or die by how their customers rate them.

At Com Tech, how lucky was I that my main competitor, Datamatic, a large listed company, had no regard for customer service? They had abused the privilege of their exclusive partnership with Novell and paid the price. From sitting on a gold mine, they went out of business, not because of the product they sold – we sold the same, identical product – but simply because of the service that they delivered to their customers. I couldn't believe it when I returned a call and a customer said, 'Thank you so much for getting back to me.' Why wouldn't I? Maybe they wanted to spend some money with me. What it told me was that Datamatic didn't even bother to return a customer call. Customers vote with their wallets: the better the service, the more they spend with you. Many years later I met the CFO of Datamatic and he told me that they used to have strategy meetings debating how we were taking so much market share. I don't know what they were strategising about. It was simple: return calls when your customers call, or they may become Com Tech customers. It wasn't just the calls – there was so much more.

Staff

Think about your ability to attract and retain the best in the industry. The better your team, the more value you will be able to add to your customers. The more value you add, the more you will sell. Remember Richard Branson: 'Employees come first.' If you believe this, make sure that you deliver. I have dedicated an entire chapter to staff later in this book.

Business partners

I have always believed that business partners are an extension of your business. In the case of Com Tech, they included our suppliers, Novell, Microsoft, Cisco, our couriers, the company that did our cabling, outside investors, everyone. If we wanted to deliver legendary customer service, sometimes we needed to rely on a third party to provide part of the service. Maybe a customer needed a product urgently – we relied on the courier to get it to the customer on time. We treated all our partners as if they worked for Com Tech and usually included them at our company kick-offs, treating them as genuine partners in our business and not just as another supplier. It really paid dividends.

Innovative performance

What are you doing this year that you didn't do last year? When Steve Jobs sadly passed away, the big concern was: 'What will happen with innovation?' Every company, big or small, has to continually reinvent themselves, each and every year. If you're still offering the same products and services that you did last year, you're going to have problems.

Every year, Com Tech took on new products – we wanted the industry to know that we had vision, that we knew where the market was going. We signed up SynOptics, the company that invented Ethernet networking over unshielded twisted pair cabling; Cisco, the market leader in wide area networking; Lotus Notes; and PictureTel for video conferencing, before it became pervasive. And we were the world's first distributor for Netscape, the company founded by Marc Andreessen.

Every year we held the Com Tech Open Systems Forum, a four-day event that became the leading networking conference in Australia. The forum was sponsored by our business partners, and customers paid to attend. It was our opportunity to show the industry our technical prowess. We had amazing speakers, including Marc Andreessen – he didn't have a passport before he came to Australia as the keynote speaker at Com Tech Open Systems Forum in 1996. It was our continual innovation in product, services and support that enabled us to lead the market from 1987 until today.

There are three types of companies:

1. Those that make things happen – **leaders**

2. Those that watch things happen – **followers**

3. Those that say, 'What happened?'
   – **the irrelevant, the dying or the dead**

You want to be the founder of a company that makes things happen and leads the industry. It's hard work – but, boy, it's so rewarding.

Many companies have become irrelevant because they did not innovate, either because they became complacent or they didn't want to disrupt their core business (like Kodak, Blockbuster and Fairfax Media). Some companies simply didn't have a strategy of continually 'innovating in innovation'.

An elite cyclist has to decide: do I lose 5 kilograms and become the world's best mountain climber, or do I gain 5 kilograms of muscle to become the world's best sprinter? Doing neither will lead to the cyclist being neither a world-class sprinter nor a world-class climber. A company is no different. You need to decide whether your company is an operationally efficient organisation or a company committed to adding value to its customers.

I believe that you get three types of companies:

OPERATIONALLY EFFICIENT	MEMORY	VALUE ADD
• Systems • People		• People • Systems

- An **operationally efficient company**, e.g. Amazon, where good people rely on world-class systems.

- A **value-add company**, e.g. McKinsey, where world-class people rely on great systems. You can't give great people lousy systems indefinitely, and you have to invest in both training your team and providing them with the systems that they need to deliver their service.

- A **memory**, a company that doesn't know whether it is operationally efficient or value add – one that doesn't invest in either its people or its systems.

Microsoft, today the world's second most valuable company, almost fell into this trap. Until the current CEO, Satya Nadella, took the helm, the company might well have been on its way to irrelevance. Like Blackberry, Novell, Fairfax and many others, Microsoft could have continued to exist for several years but would ultimately have become irrelevant. (If Blackberry dies, would anyone care?) Nadella, with the same people and products his predecessor had, turned the behemoth Microsoft on a dime to re-emerge as a dominant technology player for many years to come. So, it doesn't matter whether you have 10 people or over 100,000 people – innovate, or die.

Digital transformation/Productivity

What are you doing to make it easier:

- for your customers to do business with you, and
- for your staff to work in your company?

In a world characterised by increased competition, reduced margins and customers demanding better customer service, you can't just keep throwing people at the problem. You have to invest in systems and processes without hiring additional people – and somehow not compromise on the quality of the service delivered.

As an example, at Com Tech, by implementing a new enterprise resource planning (ERP) system, which enabled both our staff and our customers to use self-service technology to transact, we were able to double our revenues without hiring any additional sales or warehouse personnel. You may say big deal – but this was in 1992, well before the internet. I was proud of what we achieved. We went from being a distribution company with the best people in the industry and the worst systems – we ran on people power – to a company with both the best people and the best systems in the industry. While our staff were always our number one asset, you can't give great people lousy systems forever.

Cash flow and profitability

I have combined these two KPIs because – as any accountant (even a bad one like me) will tell you – if you're not profitable and generating positive cash flow, you probably won't be around for long. Sometimes you can be profitable but not cash-flow positive: you may have made some great sales, but you haven't been able to collect your cash quickly enough. Cash flow is like the blood that flows through your body – you may have the best brain, heart, lungs, liver and kidneys, but without blood flowing through your veins you cease to exist. It's the same with cash in a company.

Never has this been more applicable to a founder than when macroeconomic conditions changed in 2022 – if you can't generate cash or show a path to positive cash flow, you are probably going to go out of business.

So, when you think of the world's great companies, like Amazon, Apple, Microsoft, Google and Facebook, they tick ALL five KPI boxes. For a while Apple was seen as innovative, but until the iPod, their cash flow and profitability were poor. For many years, Microsoft was unbelievably profitable and cash-flow positive, but seemed to lack innovation. It was only when both companies excelled in all five KPI areas that they became great companies (again).

If you want your company to be great, you have to deliver on all five KPIs. Four is not good enough. You could increase your profits by laying off staff, compromising on customer service or not investing in a new product, but that's a short-term decision. Conversely, you could keep investing in R&D without commensurate levels of sales and profitability.

Managing short is managing your cash flow and profitability, while managing long is your investment in brand awareness, innovation and systems. Any good founder can manage short and any good founder can manage long, but only an exceptional founder can manage short and long at the same time. Make that your challenge!

And what about startups?

It's quite common for a startup to burn cash and *not* generate cash for some time. Facebook, Amazon and Google didn't make a profit or generate cash for years – but every company has to have a plan and path to profitability, like these three did. Today, they print money. Eventually Uber was going to have to make a buck, or it may just have become irrelevant. Under the leadership of Dan Khosrowshahi, Uber is now both profitable and cash-flow positive, and on its way to dominating the market for a global transportation system. At the same time, Zip (and lots of others) is drastically cutting costs, closing down overseas makets as it desperately changes its model of 'growth at all costs' to one of growth with sustainable profitability as the objective.

As an early-stage startup, what impacts your cash flow is your ability to raise cash from outside investors. To ensure that you can continue to fund your growth, you will have to show the positive momentum that you have generated since your last raise. What is different to last year? How many customers did you have at the last raise and how many more do you have now? Have you managed to attract new management and staff to the business? Are your existing customers spending more money with you this year than last year? Is your product better than it was at the time of your last raise?

Are you selling into international markets that you hadn't yet cracked last raise? If you can't answer yes to these questions, you may have trouble raising your next round. You have to show positive momentum in all of these five KPIs to ensure that venture capital companies are banging at your door to give you more money to get to the next stage.

● ● ●

CHAPTER 6

Crash and burn

I recently asked a young founder how he was going to make a profit. He replied, 'Dave, you have to understand that it takes time for a company to generate profits.' I answered, 'Yoav, anyone who doesn't understand that it takes time to get to profitability shouldn't be in venture capital, but any founder who doesn't understand how to make a profit and generate positive cash flow shouldn't be in business.'

When you read chapter 1, you may have thought *'This guy really is the dumbest guy at the table.'* Back at the start of this book, I asked why you would want all the aggravation, challenges and heartache of running your own business when you could earn twice as much in a job without the stress. It may not have seemed so at the time, but despite all the challenges presented by the pandemic, work from home, the toughest environment for attracting and retaining staff I have ever encountered, it was very easy to raise cash – the lifeblood of any organisation. In fact, until February 2022 it felt almost too easy to run a startup – it was a matter of growth at all costs, and you could easily raise money at a higher valuation at the next round. Then, suddenly, this situation changed.

Since about November 2021 there have been some significant changes in the macroeconomic environment that have led to higher-than-expected inflation, which has resulted in Central Banks imposing higher interest rates. This in turn has resulted in a massive fall in the valuation of stock prices – particularly growth stocks. The tech-heavy NASDAQ exchange fell by more than 25 per cent between January and June 2022, with some stocks falling as much as 90 per cent from their previous highs. The impact on public markets had to filter through to the private markets. After all, your exit is ultimately either an IPO where there's been a massive valuation reset, or a trade sale where your acquirer's valuation has probably taken a massive hit too.

Many of our founders had never lived through a recession nor experienced the effect that higher interest rates would have on their valuations and, importantly, on their ability to raise cash (see my email to our founders on page 213). Prior to this, as I've mentioned above, startups were encouraged to grow at all costs. Profitability was almost seen as a negative, and as long as you were growing your revenues, you would probably be able to raise cash at a higher valuation at the next round.

I always went by the mantra, 'revenue is vanity, profitability is sanity'. For a while, I thought that the traditional way of operating a business had run its course and then – CRASH – it suddenly changed. If you couldn't keep growing – profitably, or at least with profitability in sight – you weren't going to be able to raise cash, and all your hard work was going to go down the gurgler. To survive, you would have to reduce your burn and extend your cash runway to give yourself the best chance of making it through. Now, more than ever, a founder had to have the edge in order to make those very tough Yes and No decisions. It didn't matter whether you were Mark Zuckerberg at Meta, Elon Musk at Twitter, Andy Jassy at Amazon or – closer to home – Zip, Atlassian and others. Somehow you had to make shit taste like chocolate.

Capital efficiency is key

Founders now had to work out how to do more with less: 'What percentage of my staff am I going to have to let go, which offices am I closing down, what products need to go, how much can I reduce my marketing spend without impacting revenue growth, which perks are coming to an end – and how will all of this affect our culture? Google can provide free massages and lunch to staff because they print money – now I'm going to have to learn that I will only be able to attract and retain staff by using the skills identified in the diagram on page 106 of this book.' Today, capital efficiency is key to the survival of any startup, and founders will have to focus on how much revenue every dollar of cost will generate. If you're not capital efficient, your cash will soon be gone and a venture capital firm won't be willing to back you – they will be worried that you just don't know how to make a buck.

I always say that I learnt more *outside* of my curriculum than I did during my formal lectures while studying accounting. One of the best lessons came from my accounting lecturer, Prof. McGregor. 'The reason so many companies fail is that their founders don't even know what their break-even point is – they have no idea what it costs to open the doors every month.' When I started Com Tech, these words rang in my ears every day. *How much do I have to sell just to pay the bills?* If my gross profit (unit economics) was 25 per cent and it cost me $50,000 to open my doors every month, what was the likelihood that I could sell $200,000 per month? If my gross profit dropped to 20 per cent, then I would have to sell $250,000 just to pay the bills. If I hired a new staff member for $10,000 per month, how confident was I that I would generate an extra $40,000 just to pay the salary?

While you can never be 100 per cent certain, I always wanted to give myself the best chance of success. Before Novell appointed me as a distributor, the Novell country manager Peter Stanford said that he couldn't sign me as a distributor with our humble little office in Erskine Street – we would need to sign a lease for an office more befitting of a distributor of the world's leading network operating system. I found premises in Doody Street, Alexandria ... still called Com Tech Communications Centre and currently home to Australian tech success story WiseTech Global. I showed Peter the premises and said, 'Sign me as a distributor and I will sign the lease.' I knew I could pay the bills with a Novell distribution agreement, but I would have gone out of business without one.

I missed realising my dream because of avoidable mistakes

I want to share a few examples of some of the mistakes that I have seen founders make, mostly rookie errors that could easily have been avoided. To make matters worse, in each of the cases discussed below, the original business thesis was still valid. It was silly mistakes that got the founders into the situation that they now faced. I did say that business is not easy – but while I always gravitate to empathetic leaders like Satya Nadella (Microsoft CEO) and Bob Iger (Disney CEO), being empathetic doesn't mean you don't make the tough calls.

As a partner in a founder-friendly VC fund, I have learnt a lot. I always say you can't afford to be reckless in either direction – and we made the mistake of advising our founders on what steps they should take to survive, but recklessly were too soft in not enforcing the implementation of these changes. In fact, we have occasionally let our founders down by not being more aggressive about the value that our experience could provide ... instead of being founder friendly, we have been, in some cases, founder foolish.

I want to make it clear that I don't think I know everything. Irrespective of my past experience of building Com Tech into the company that it was, and despite trying to follow my own set of rules for building a long-term sustainable company, I have not been immune from failure myself. In 2014 I became chairman of a public company called MOQ Digital. This despite vowing never to get involved with a public company – nor a company that generated the bulk of its revenues from professional services. It's a good rule to never do what you don't want to do – follow your gut! MOQ had amazing customer and staff satisfaction and was extremely highly regarded by our main business partner, Microsoft. We just didn't know how to make a buck. Our unit economics never stacked up, and despite a great team and happy customers, in November 2022, after eight years of persevering, we faced up to the reality that we simply didn't know how to build a long-term sustainable business. We ended up selling the company to Brennan IT at way less than anticipated by the original investors – including myself and some of the founders who sold their business into the dream of building a national Microsoft Cloud services company. I felt that I had personally let down a lot of people: shareholders; staff; and, most importantly, the founders of the companies that we had acquired along the way, who had vended their good companies into MOQ with the expectation of being a smaller part of something great.

Case A: Failure to cut costs soon enough cost me my business

We identified that 90 per cent of revenue was being generated by 10 per cent of the costs. We advised the founder to get rid of the 90 per cent of costs that generated the 10 per cent of revenue. The founder convinced us that a global footprint was necessary for the future of the business. We trusted the founder. The founder ran out of runway and lost most of his equity.

Case B: Face reality as it is, not as it was or you wish it to be.

While the stock market was tanking, a founder wanted to raise capital at five times the valuation of the previous round, despite the fact the business hadn't changed much since the last raise and, even worse, the market for the category of service being offered had fallen about 90 per cent. We advised the founder to try to raise through an extension of the last round raise – that would be a great outcome. An advisor told the founder that the five times valuation was fair. I suggested that the founder suggest that the advisor put his money where his mouth was. And how much did that advisor contribute to the raise? You guessed it: not a cent. Nine months after trying to raise at this ridiculous valuation, the founder was willing to take money at half the last round's valuation. Nine months wasted. Instead of selling and winning business, the founder was wasting valuable time trying to raise capital at a valuation that didn't reflect current market conditions. I hope that the founder succeeds – it would be well deserved.

Case C: To climb Kilimanjaro, you first have to get to base camp

An outstanding tech founder, advised by a director who doubled up as an acting CEO because of his perceived expertise, was led to invest in people and infrastructure way ahead of time. This was clearly a case of a board of directors trying to run the company instead of assisting the founder to find a complementary front-of-house COO to help maximise the potential of an enormous opportunity (see the later chapter on directors). Capital efficiency is key in any business, but in today's environment it is critical. Instead of focusing on one or two verticals, they attacked everything, delivered on nothing and moved internationally way before they were ready. Instead of investing wisely and conserving their most valuable resource – cash – they burnt through the cash and have put a potentially great business in jeopardy. Honestly, my heart bleeds for the amazing founder.

Case D: Are my unit economics sufficient to eventually make a buck?

Two young founders told me that their business was going great. They had grown the number of experiences they were selling by tenfold. The founders were generating $30,000 of revenue and spending $130,000 per month. Each experience generated $30 of revenue. *Guys, you need to sell 4333 ($130,000 / 30) experiences a month just to pay the bills. You are currently selling 1000. Come back when you can show me that you have a realistic chance of achieving this, and then I will tell you whether the business is going great.* They valued my input!

At risk of sounding arrogant: my colleagues in the VC fund and I don't know everything, but we are able to provide valuable business advice. After all, as my partner Geoff Levy says, that's why you want to work with people who have no hair (Geoff) or grey hair (me).

— — —

Earlier in this chapter I mentioned that I learnt more outside of my curriculum than I did during my accounting course. When I graduated, the gentleman who made the commencement speech was the person who had brought Toyota to South Africa, Albert Wessels. He said: 'In my lifetime, there have been eight recessions and seven booms, so I guess we're heading for another boom.' So the encouraging news is that while the good times don't last forever, nor do the bad times. Those founders who navigate successfully during this period will be rewarded with a better business, less competition and the satisfaction of knowing that they are well on the way to building a long-term sustainable company – one that meets ALL five KPIs articulated in the previous chapter.

● ● ●

Today capital efficiency is key to the survival of any startup, and founders will have to focus on how much revenue every dollar of cost will generate.

CHAPTER 7

Taking care of business partners

As I have said before, a good partnership works when both parties add value to each other.

At Com Tech I knew what I expected from the suppliers that we worked with, and at the same time I recognised what they should expect from us as their distribution partner in Australia.

To keep the two triangles equal, I needed my suppliers to provide us with an industry-standard, market-leading product. If anything changed, the triangle would no longer be balanced. This happened on many occasions during my tenure as founder of Com Tech. The toughest one was telling Novell that I was going to sign a distribution agreement with Novell's arch-enemy, Microsoft. Novell had put me on the map, given me the opportunity of a lifetime and had helped to make Com Tech the company that we were.

What should you expect from a partner who sells your product?

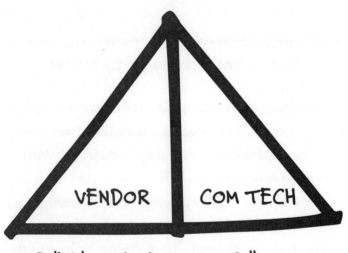

VENDOR
- Reliable product
- Market leader

COM TECH
- Sell
- Support
- Pay

When I signed with Novell in 1989, they were the dominant player in local area networking – commanding 70 per cent market share. They were growing 40 per cent year on year and so were we. By 1996, that market share had been severely eroded by Microsoft. At that stage, we were the exclusive distributor for Novell. In 1989, the biggest risk to our business was that we were one of four Novell distributors in Australia – all selling an identical product into the Australian marketplace. The only way that we could differentiate ourselves was by the people selling and supporting their products. By 1996, the biggest risk to our business was that we had become Novell's exclusive distributor – all the others had disappeared. Microsoft was killing Novell, and if we didn't sign a distribution agreement with Microsoft we would become irrelevant. Novell was dying and we didn't have to die with them. The triangle was no longer balanced – Novell added no value to Com Tech.

Although by nature I'm a very loyal person, I signed with Microsoft. I wasn't going to let down the 240 people who worked at Com Tech. I was the CEO of Com Tech – Novell's problems were *their* problems; I couldn't make their problems *our* problems. In 1989, Novell was 80 per cent of our business. When I left in 2001, it accounted for 0.8 per cent of our business. If we hadn't made that change,

Com Tech would not have achieved the outcome that we did when we sold for an enterprise value of over $1 billion. Sometimes the right decision is the hardest decision. I said that a founder has to have the edge to make those tough Yes or No decisions.

So, if we expected our vendors to keep investing in product and marketing to ensure that they retained their dominant market position, what should they have expected from us? When someone appoints you as their partner, they are essentially outsourcing a part of their business that they could have done themselves. You outsource because you believe that party is going to do at least as good a job as you would have done for the parts of your business you've entrusted them to carry out on your behalf.

To keep our vendors happy, we needed to:

1. sell lots of their product,

2. support the product as well as they would, and

3. pay our bills on time.

It was no use doing two out of three, we had to deliver on all three. Say our budget with Cisco was $100 million. If we did $70 million, provided legendary support for their product and paid our bills on time – we had let them down. We had missed our budget by $30 million. Likewise, it would have been no use doing $130 million, going broke and then being unable to pay our outstanding bills. Partnerships work when BOTH parties deliver on all of their commitments. That's how you keep the triangle balanced.

Afterpay has been a massive success, both with retailers and their customers. Retailers can see that by using Afterpay their basket size and conversion rates grow, while the end customer loves getting access to their purchase without having to lay out all the cash up front. Simple, but beneficial to both parties.

As a founder, you need to constantly assess what you expect from your partners and what your partner expects from you. When both sides deliver on their obligations, partnerships work.

● ● ●

CHAPTER 8

Legendary customer service

At Com Tech, we were always competitor aware but customer obsessive.

I don't want to say that we ran Com Tech with blinkers on, but it's hard enough worrying about your own company – if you have to worry about everything that your competition is doing, you will never sleep. When I started, I was determined to be the best technology company in Australia. If I just wanted to be 1 per cent better than my direct competitor, Datamatic, I would also have been a lousy company. To me, in the late 1980s Compaq Computers was the benchmark, and so I set my goal as having our customers regard Com Tech as better than Compaq.

Customer service is the provision of service to customers before, during and after selling something

You only know how good your supplier is when the shit hits the fan. How do they respond when things go wrong? This is a supplier's opportunity to shine.

I once saw a *60 Minutes* episode about Las Vegas, in which the program's host said, 'This place hasn't been built on winners, this place has been built on losers.' I always say that Com Tech was built on problems and on our ability to solve those problems as and when they occurred. To this day, before I ever sell something to a customer, I always present the diagram below. I refer to it as the Valley of Death.

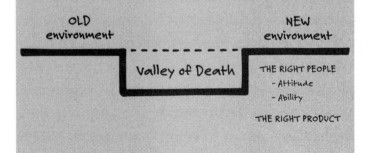

to them. Do this well and the sales will flow. Do it poorly at your peril.

I would tell customers before they bought from me: 'We're going to have problems. They may be ours, they may be yours, they may be the product that we are using, or they may even be related to a third party – but we're going to have issues. That's why you want to work with us. When we have problems, there will be no finger pointing – we're all sitting on the same side of the table.'

I think we've all been around long enough to know that technology is fraught with problems. I've worked with almost every major large vendor, and I've also been involved with many smaller companies like Holly and MacromatiX – and there are always issues. How often have you received a new version of your iPhone software that fixes some bug?

Our job at Com Tech was to take our customers from an old computer environment to a new computer environment, as painlessly as possible. When we hit that Valley of Death, I knew that not only were we working with the right products, but – just as importantly – we had the people with both the ability AND the attitude to fix those problems as and when they occurred. We always did fix them. I can honestly say that we never let a customer down, and it's how we built our brand and our profits too.

For many years, Macquarie Bank never bought product from us – they purchased directly from the vendors instead, as they believed that Com Tech could add no value. That was, until they moved from their Bond Street office to their new head office at 1 Martin Place. They moved over a weekend, and when everyone showed up for work on the Monday, nothing worked. Mac Bank was deep in that Valley of Death. Cisco was blaming Novell for the outage and Novell was blaming Cisco. In desperation, the CIO, Rob Hamlin, called me and told me that this was our opportunity to add value. I sent one of the best tech guys that I have ever worked with, Roland Chia, to fix the problem. Within a few minutes, Rollie had isolated the issue. He had switched off the Novell network and the network still didn't work. It was a Cisco problem. As soon as Cisco acknowledged that it was their problem, they threw everything at it. If you were going to have problems, you wanted to have Cisco as your supplier – like us, they were fanatical about customer service. Rob Hamlin was impressed, and Rollie's outstanding work won us many millions of dollars of business with Mac Bank after we saved the day.

Conversely, poor customer service can be catastrophic for a business. I witnessed this once when I went down to Melbourne with my colleague and longtime business partner Dave Jacobson. We were going to Melbourne to see Telstra – together with our partner, SynOptics – to sign a massive contract for Ethernet hubs. SynOptics was the pioneer and market leader in Ethernet networking over unshielded twisted pair cable. Together with SynOptics' country manager and their sales manager, Dave and I were meeting with the infamous Mariyon Skreblin and John (Giovanni) Vilani, two of the toughest negotiators I have ever dealt with.

Mariyon's EA had offered us coffee – but Mariyon said, 'Forget the coffee, bring the champagne.' We sat down, and without any preliminary discussion Mariyon simply signed the contract. The trouble was that the contract included a product that Telstra had not requested. Rather than the current version of the Ethernet hub listed in the contract, Telstra were expecting the *next* version, which had additional and important features required by Telstra. SynOptics would have had to ship two units instead of one until the new version was available. This would have been costly for SynOptics.

The contract was signed, and the SynOptics country manager never said a word. I whispered under my breath, 'Tell Mariyon about the issue.' He didn't say anything, so I said it again. When he still did nothing, I said, 'Mariyon, the contract that you have signed does not include the next generation of hubs, but we do have a solution until it becomes available.' Fuming, Mariyon ripped up the contract and said, 'Get out.' When Dave and I stood up to leave, he told us, 'Not you.' He thanked us for our honesty.

It cost SynOptics and Com Tech at least $10 million over the years, and Hewlett Packard became the incumbent supplier to Telstra. The country manager rightly got fired! Com Tech still did lots of business with Telstra, but Mariyon was true to his word: SynOptics – and then Bay Networks, the company formed by the merger of SynOptics and Wellfleet – never did business with Australia's largest customer again. I was proud to receive an email from Mariyon when he resigned from Telstra, saying that no other supplier had the integrity that we did. Coming from Mariyon, that was a big compliment. You can lose money, lots of it, but you can't lose your reputation, not a shred of it!

Problems don't just occur with technology. A bad meal served at a restaurant, the wrong package delivered by a supplier, or a flight delayed by an airline – how you respond to these problems will determine the difference between an ordinary company and a great company.

I was lucky enough to work with two outstanding founders at Centric Wealth, Jon Pillemer and Roy

Agranat. They ran the risk and life insurance practice. You don't want to know how good your provider is when it comes to life insurance – it means that you're in trouble. Either you have passed away and your loved ones need to claim on your policy, or you have suffered major trauma. When it came to these types of tragedies, there was no small print with Jonny and Roy. I saw how they fought to ensure that their customers' policies were honoured to the letter, to make certain that families didn't suffer any additional trauma or avoidable distress. Take the case of one of Jonny's clients, who had terminal cancer. The client wanted to know that his family would be provided for once he had passed. Somehow, Jonny convinced the insurance provider to pay the policy prior to the client's death, giving the man peace of mind before he passed away. I haven't worked with Jonny and Roy for years, but I continue to recommend them to everyone, because I know how they fight for their clients when they most need the help. Jonny and Roy have a thriving business today (Fairbridge Wealth) – not surprising, considering their obsession with customer satisfaction.

I could continue writing about customer service for several more chapters – yes, I always have been and always will be obsessed with customer service. Just like my builder, Ron Conti. I met Ron in 2000, through a referral from my now business partner, Geoff Levy. When I asked Ron about the way he liked to work, he said, 'David, it's got to be fair for you and fair for me.' I shook his hand, and that was our contract. Eighteen years later I was building again and who was I using? Ron Conti. I still didn't have a contract. I think that between 2003 and now, Ron would have got at least six large jobs on my recommendation – as I've said before, there is no better salesperson than a happy customer. During the 13 years that I lived in my last house, if there was ever an issue, Ron would be there in a heartbeat. And he never gave me a bill. I found it almost embarrassing to call him.

In 2018, when I was organising a cycling tour to Italy for myself and my mates, I was lucky enough to meet a delightful couple, Daniel and Tara Brickell. Their company, Chameleon Bike Adventures, took 16 of us to Italy. They went above and beyond to make sure that it was an unforgettable cycling experience in Italy – not just a cycling trip. The little things they did made such a massive difference. If you want to go cycling in Italy, call Dan and Tara, they won't let you down.

It doesn't matter whether you are a one-man band like Conti Construction, or a two-person company like Chameleon Bike Adventures, legendary customer

A perfect customer partnership

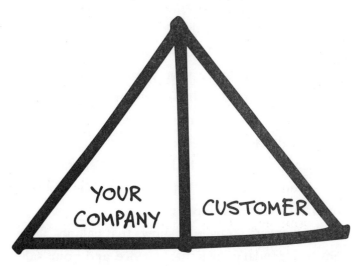

YOUR COMPANY

- Great product
- Legendary customer service
  - Accurate info
  - A prompt response
- Don't keep customers in the dark
  - Bad news doesn't get better with time!

CUSTOMER

- Buy lots
- Pay on time
- Refer other customers

service (or, in the case of Amazon, fanatical customer service) will always be the differentiator in your business.

At the end of the day, providing legendary customer service is pretty simple. All that customers expect is accurate information, a prompt response and not being kept in the dark – bad news doesn't get better with time. I don't know what the country manager of SynOptics was thinking. As soon as Telstra had received their first shipment, they would have realised that the latest version of the product was unavailable. I'm pretty sure that if the country manager had explained the issue, Telstra would have been more than happy – and the contract would not have been ripped up.

The diagram on page 75 shows that balance again. Deliver legendary customer service and your sales with existing customers will grow, while attracting business from new customers will become easier.

● ● ●

You can lose money, lots of it, but you can't lose your reputation, not a shred of it!

CHAPTER 9

Oh, Mother, should I work with my brother?

So, I've founded a company. What's the story about bringing in family?

Any person who joins your company should be there because they are going to add value to the business – this is even more applicable when it comes to family.

You can't afford to build a company where people in the company feel that the only reason James is here is because he is Jane's husband, or that the only reason that Jim is in the business is because he is the founder's son. You can't build a great company when your team thinks that the only way anyone can get anywhere in the business is if they're a family member. You can only succeed when your team knows that any career opportunity is based on merit and on the value that they add, no matter their name, gender, religion or race. Why would any sensible founder not want to promote the best? Sometimes common sense is not common practice.

I worked at Com Tech with my two older brothers: Jon joined after a year and Steven after about two years. Like Dad, we were all chartered accountants. How could we possibly add value if we were all accountants? Well, you get accountants ... and then you get accountants – and only one of us was really qualified to do the books. When we eventually brought in Macquarie Bank as a private equity partner, the Mac Bank board representative, Michael Traill, affectionately referred to us as Doom, Gloom and Boom.

Steve was Doom. He predicted the global financial crisis 25 years before it happened. He was a real CFO, and truly safeguarded the assets of the company. Steve is by nature extremely conservative, and he was always negative about Com Tech expanding into new areas of business and new regions, constantly questioning how we would fund our growth.

Jon was Boom. He only ever saw blue sky. When things were tough – even in great companies, you have your challenges – Jon still only ever envisioned a positive outcome.

I was Gloom – even when things were going brilliantly, I was always worrying about something. Who could disrupt our business? What could we be doing better for our staff and customers?

We were an awesome combination, especially Jon and I.

Steve prepared our management accounts with amazing diligence and managed our inventory and accounts receivables. As a distribution company, at times we may have had $250 million tied up in these assets – poor management could have cost us our business. Our industry was rife with bad debts and obsolete inventory. Steve kept ours to a minimum.

Jon worried about today, and I worried about tomorrow. I may have had the vision, but Jon executed on my vision better than I would have done myself. I was the hunter, Jon the farmer. I would identify a new product and then the challenge for me was to secure the distribution rights. Once I had achieved that objective, someone needed to manage the partnership. There was nobody better than Jon. Our suppliers loved him and he was able to negotiate discounts that really helped our profit margins – as my dad taught us from an early age: 'Boys, the profit is made in the buying, not the selling.'

Despite all three of us being accountants, there was very little – if any – overlap between us. Jon focused on merchandising (ordering inventory) and sales, while my focus was marketing and sales. So, admittedly, we *did* overlap on sales – but you can never have enough of that. If an account manager wanted me to visit a customer and I was busy, they would take Jon, and vice versa. We also both invested heavily in enhancing our staff relationships – which, I can't emphasise enough, is a critical role for any leader.

With minimal overlap in our respective roles, my brothers and I all added significant value to Com Tech – and I know that I'm right about that. After I left, Jon remained in the company for about six months, then became an advisor and continued as a board member for many years. Steve stayed on as financial director for another six years. If they were both there only because they were my brothers, Dimension Data would have fired them the day that I left. They must have added value.

Once I left Com Tech, we never worked together again. While I'm sure that Jon and I have both done well independently, I have no doubt that we would have done better as a combination. Just as Lillee and Thommo or Horan and Little were to sport, we were the best combination in the industry in 2000. But we didn't maximise the opportunity presented by the internet – something that two other brothers, Paul and Andrew Bassat of SEEK fame, absolutely nailed. We should have continued on our path.

Some family members may not work directly in the business but even so are an essential part of it – and I'm talking about your life partner.

As a founder, I would not have been able to achieve what I did without the unbelievable support I got from my wife, Colleen. We have three sons, and the amount of time and effort that Colleen put into raising our boys was huge. My boys are good kids, but sometimes on a Monday I would think, *Phew, work today!* Being a stay-at-home mum is a full-time job. While Colleen never came into the office, her role often involved entertaining staff, suppliers and customers at our home or at restaurants. Being a founder is tough – not having a supportive partner makes it that much harder again.

Colleen never thought I would quit. However, I always said that one day someone would come knocking on our door wanting to buy Com Tech. I knew that as long as we were building a great company, we would always have options. We were on a rocket ship and it would have been irresponsible of me to get off – I had the opportunity to set my family up financially for life. I was realistic enough to know that without the lucky breaks I'd had when founding Com Tech I would probably never get that opportunity again. Fourteen years was worth the sacrifice. Thanks to Colleen, our sons are all great, hard-working, well-rounded boys. We are able to do things as a family that we may not have been able to do if Colleen and I hadn't put in those fourteen years of hard yakka.

A few years ago, Colleen and I were able to share this advice with one of Australia's most successful founders and his wife. I think they sincerely valued the guidance at the time, and they found it encouraging to know that you can have both a successful startup *and* a great marriage – they are not mutually exclusive.

● ● ●

You can only succeed when your team knows that any career opportunity is based on merit.

CHAPTER 10

Who's important in a company?

You can't win a rugby game with great forwards and lousy backs, and you don't win a cricket test with great bowlers and poor batters.

To succeed, you need both – it's that simple. Similarly, you can't win in business without amazing sales, admin and technical people, all working together as a team. To build an inclusive culture, you must value everyone's role equally. Everyone should know that they have an important part to play in the success of the business, no matter where they work in the company. Whether they pack a box in a warehouse, answer a phone at reception, work in sales, customer success or marketing, or are a full-stack software developer, everyone plays a key role.

No matter your role, everyone is important in a company

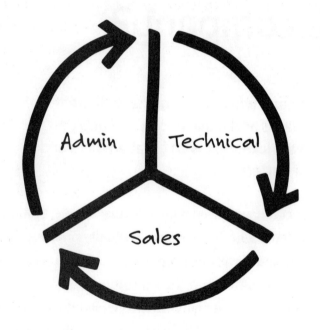

Valuing people means respect for the person and the role – it doesn't mean paying everyone equally. Obviously, market forces will determine what salaries you need to pay to attract and retain the best people for the positions they serve.

At Com Tech, I used to make the mistake of saying: 'Our salespeople aren't the most important people in the company – it's our technical and admin teams that help us win and keep the business.' I managed to piss off the sales guys by saying this – and they were certainly right to feel that way. So I changed what I said to: 'Our salespeople are critical, but no more critical than our tech and admin teams.' It worked.

We also put our money where our mouth was – we paid generous bonuses to everyone in the company, and I mean generous. I will never forget receiving a $50 Christmas bonus when I was at Price Waterhouse. I almost wanted to give it back ... I didn't know that things were so tough at the firm. Seriously, what could I do with $50, even in 1985? At Com Tech, we paid double and triple salary cheques to our star performers, irrespective of where they worked in the company. If you went above and beyond, you were rewarded handsomely. And yes, some people may have received a triple bonus cheque and some nothing. Not all people are created equal. Those who went above and beyond were treated differently to those who just did their job – for that, you get a salary.

When it came to our company kick-off, every member of the company was there. If everyone truly is important in a company, everyone has to be at events like this. I could never understand how companies would have a president's club just for their top-performing salespeople, when so much of each sale was done by project managers, tech engineers and the admin team. It was never just a salesperson who won a deal – every opportunity that we ever won involved a team effort.

However, I'll confess, it was only once I got involved as an investor in startups that were building their own products that I realised why the US-based companies Com Tech partnered with gave so much prestige to their sales teams. As a distributor of an industry-standard, market-leading product like Microsoft or Apple, we were merely fulfilling demand. I will never forget walking into the office of the branch manager of IBM in Canberra and there, hanging on his wall, was a huge poster: 'Nothing happens until you sell something'. The penny had dropped: no matter how good your product, until you get that product to market – and no matter the growth method, whether a sales-led strategy, a marketing-led growth strategy or a product-led growth strategy – you have to get people buying and using your product. This is the only way that you generate revenues. And, just as importantly, your product goes from v1.0 to v2.0 etc. as you receive valuable feedback from the people your product was designed to serve – customers.

Obviously, technical people don't exist only in the IT industry. Technical people are everywhere. In a media company they are your journalists, in a fashion house they are the designers and at a restaurant they are the chefs. It's no use providing great service at a restaurant if the kitchen is serving up substandard food– it won't be long before you're out of business.

At Com Tech, I was always convinced that the strength of the pack is the wolf and the strength of the wolf is the pack. I was so obsessed about the power of the team that at different times I included two Australian sporting greats on our board. If anyone knew about a team, it was Bob Dwyer, Australia's 1991 Rugby World Cup winning coach, who sat on our board between 1989 and 1995 (when he left to coach Leicester in the UK). When I asked Bob to sit on our board, he told me that he had no skills in technology. I told him that we had enough of those. I wanted someone who had his values and understood the power of teamwork.

I have personal experience of those values. Having had too many drinks at a Randwick rugby season opening event we were both attending, I approached Bob and asked if he could send my dad – an avid rugby supporter – a fax to tell him that if he wanted to watch a decent team playing rugby, he should come and live in Australia (it was 1988, when there was no email). Given the circumstances, I didn't think anything more of it – until my father rang me from South Africa to ask about the fax he'd just received from the coach of the Australian rugby team. Bob had heard me out and honoured his word. These were the values I wanted to build for Com Tech: what we said we'd do, we did – our actions matched our words. At the end of Bob's coaching career, Australia's greatest rugby player, John Eales, was asked to say a few words at Bob's book launch. I remember John saying: 'Bob didn't just teach us how to play rugby, Bob taught us how to be gentlemen. He would say, "I don't care if you have signed 500 autographs for the day and a kid asks you for your signature – that may be the only contact that kid ever has with a Wallaby. Make sure that it is a positive experience."' These were the values that I wanted for our company – any contact with our company should be a positive experience.

When Bob left for the UK in 1995, legendary Australian cricket captain and batsman, Ian Chappell (who kindly wrote the foreword for this book) joined our board.

I appointed Bob and Ian because of the people they are – no egos, team players, always looking to see how they could add value to our staff, customers and business partners – *not* because of the status that they command. The fact that Ian and Bob are both legends, in their respective fields, was simply a bonus.

Both Bob and Ian added significant value in their own way, and I'm proud to still be mates with them. They are two of Australia's finest!

● ● ●

The First XV

15 All Black Principles

Summarised from James Kerr, *Legacy*, 2015. Whether you like rugby or not, I highly recommend that if you care about culture, you read this book. The All Blacks are the most successful professional sporting team in history, with a winning percentage of about 80 per cent.

1. Sweep the sheds
Never be too big to do the small things that need to be done
Before leaving the dressing room at the end of the game, all the players stop and tidy up. They literally and figuratively 'sweep the sheds', an example of personal humility, a cardinal All Blacks value.

2. Go for the gap
When you're on top of your game, change your game
The philosophy of and focus on continual improvement and continuous learning leaves no room for complacency.

3. Play with purpose
Ask 'why?'
Better people make better All Blacks is a core belief, and understanding 'why?' identifies the purpose of being an All Black. The power of purpose galvanises individuals in an organisation – what's the purpose of yours?

4. Pass the ball

Leaders create leaders

Shared responsibility means shared ownership; a sense of inclusion serves to unite individuals, and collaboration means advancement as a team.

5. Create a learning environment

Leaders are learners

For the All Blacks, leaders are learners and teachers. As Jack Hobbs, former captain, said: *Get up every day and be the best you can be. Never let the music die in you.*

6. No dickheads

Follow the Whānau

The All Blacks select on character over talent, which means some promising players never pull on the black jersey, because they don't have the right character.

7. Embrace expectations

Aim for the highest cloud

A culture of expectation enables the asking and re-asking of fundamental questions: how can we do better? Taking risks and responsibilities is one of the skills you learn from rugby, a contest of strength, skills and intelligence.

NO ONE IS BIGGER THAN THE TEAM. THE TEAM ALWAYS COMES FIRST.

HUMILITY, RESPECT, EXCELLENCE

8. Train to win
Practise under pressure
The philosophy means finding ways to do more by preparation and practice. There's a Māori saying: the way the sapling is shaped determines how the tree grows.

9. Keep a blue head
Control your attention
One minute can decide the outcome of a game, as it can the outcome of a business situation. Avoiding poor decision-making under pressure is vital.

10. Know thyself
Keep it real
Honesty drives better performance. Attributed to Socrates, the phrase 'know thyself' is a key tenet of All Blacks philosophy, believing that development of the authentic self is essential to performance.

11. Invent your own language
Sing your world into existence
It's a system of meaning that everyone understands, a language and vocabulary, a set of beliefs that bind the group.

12. Sacrifice
Find something you would die for and give your life to it
Don't be a good All Black, be a great All Black. Give everything you have – then a little bit more.

13. Ritualise to actualise

Create a culture

Rituals reflect, remind and reinforce the belief system, to reignite collective identity and purpose.

Au, Au, Aue Bā! – It's our time. It's our moment! The final line of Haka.

14. Be a good ancestor

Plant trees you'll never see

As the sun shines on you, on this moment, this is your time. It's your obligation and responsibility to add the legacy – to leave the jersey in a better place. The legacy is more intimidating than any opposition.

15. Write your legacy

This is your time

When a player makes the All Blacks, they're given a small black book. The first page shows a jersey from the 1905 Originals, the first tour. On the next page is another jersey, that of the 1924 Invincibles, and thereafter, pages of other jerseys, until the present day. The rest of the pages are blank, waiting to be filled by the player himself.

MANY OF US ARE MORE CAPABLE THAN SOME OF US, BUT NONE OF US IS AS CAPABLE AS ALL OF US. THE ALL BLACKS SHOW IT IN EVERY GAME. MAKE SURE YOUR BUSINESS HAS THIS HEART BEAT TOO.

CHAPTER 11

Superstars, dogs, non-performing team players – and those brilliant jerks

During my time in management, I have observed that people always fall into one of four categories.

1. **Superstars**, who meet their objectives and share the values of the company.

2. **Dogs**, who neither meet their objectives nor share the values of the company.

3. **Non-performing team players**, who share the values of the company but do not meet their objectives.

4. **Brilliant jerks**, who meet their objectives but do not share the values of the company.

Dealing with superstars and dogs is in fact really easy. Make sure that you do whatever it takes

FOUR KINDS OF PEOPLE

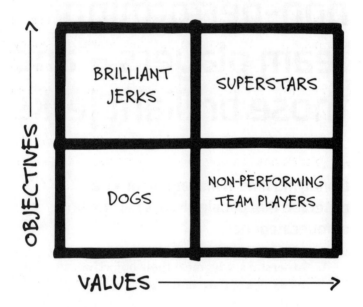

to keep the superstars, and get rid of the dogs as quickly as possible.

With wages probably your largest monthly expense, being able to both grow *and* keep your star performers is critical. Losing a star performer can leave a massive void in a company. Research shows that replacing a star performer can cost a business two to three times the worker's salary. Star performers can deliver 400 per cent more in productivity than your average employee, so losing a star can have a massive impact on your ability to build your product and generate revenue. A replacement can take months to get to the same level of performance as the high-performing employee – as a startup, you just don't have this kind of time on your side.

Because I considered Com Tech as a family, I always worried that if I asked someone to leave the company – even a dog – it may have a negative impact on our culture. How wrong I was. I believe I sometimes lost respect as a manager because I didn't make the tough decisions soon enough. My strong recommendation is always to be fair first and tough second – but don't err on the fair side for too long, a mistake I often made.

Whenever I held a management meeting, I would ask our managers to think of a situation where they had believed someone was not the right person for the company but had allowed them to stay on, rather than removing them. Had they ever found themselves, two years down the track, saying: 'Lucky I never got rid of Jack, he has become an absolute superstar'? Never in my career have I known that to happen. When you know something is not right, it's not right. Think about your own career – can you think of anyone like that?

Non-performing team players are the second-toughest group to deal with – maybe a salesperson who missed their number for a quarter, or a software engineer who has bugs in their software. They are great company people, but haven't met their KPIs or OKRs (objectives and key results) or whatever system you use to manage your team. You have to give this team player another go and see whether you can educate them, to help get them into the top right quadrant of the diagram on page 100. If you can't, it's probably best for them and the company that you part ways.

The toughest group that a manager has to deal with are those brilliant jerks – they may include your best salesperson or your most competent engineer, but these people are not willing to be part of the team. They just don't fit the culture. Think of a star footballer, someone who believes they are so good they don't have to attend practice, so special they don't need to wear the team kit when travelling – but hey, this is your champion player. You may think your company can't survive without this person, but your culture won't survive with this brilliant jerk on board. You lose credibility as a founder if you are willing to let someone do whatever they want even when it is contrary to the values of the company. As hard as it is, this person has to go – no one is bigger than the team.

Recently I was invited to be guest speaker for a company in the real estate industry. Their star performer didn't pitch up for the management meeting and dinner on the Monday night. The conference kicked off at 10 am on the Tuesday, and the brilliant jerk arrived at ... 10.15. What example was this setting for the rest of the company? Why did everyone need to be there at 10 am if the brilliant jerk could arrive whenever he wanted? He's no longer with the company. I know the founder was a bit apprehensive about letting him go, but I'm confident that in a few years he will look back on it as one of the best decisions that he has made.

I should add that a brilliant jerk in one company may be a superstar in another – every company has its own unique culture.

● ● ●

CHAPTER 12

It's all about people

So, we now know that everyone is important in a company, no matter what their role. Staff engagement is directly linked to customer satisfaction, profitability and innovation.

Many managers think that salary is the key motivator for attracting and retaining staff. But money doesn't buy loyalty – although of course it's a factor. What actually encourages good employees to stay is the authentic personal connections made between managers and staff. What is key today is that the relationships require empathetic leadership – think Satya Nadella at Microsoft! I have always been an empathetic leader, and it has stood me in good stead.

Motivated staff put in extra effort, demonstrate their commitment to stay and, importantly, act as the best lead source for new staff referrals. So, one of the most critical roles for a founder is to attract and retain

The perfect company-employee partnership

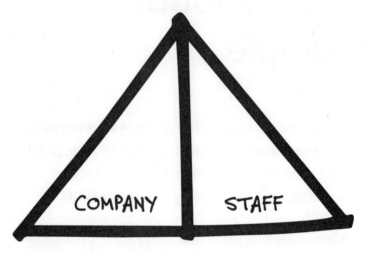

COMPANY

- Good remuneration

- Job satisfaction
  - Appreciated
  - Promoted
  - Challenged
  - Training

- Input
  - Listened to
  - Involved in decision making

STAFF

- Legendary customer service

- Team player

- Value add
  - Not how many hours you work
  - Not how long you have been with the company
  - It's your contribution that counts

superstars – people who both meet their objectives and share the values of the company. How do we do it?

Remember what I learnt from my first job in Australia. If I didn't like the fact that I was poorly paid, had no job satisfaction and wasn't allowed any input into how to fulfil my role, then other people would probably react the same way. When recruiting a team, always consider all three of these key requirements in order to keep staff happy. Remember, it's not just about attracting, it's about retaining, too – it's about continually investing in your number one asset. Never lose sight of that.

I once presented at a not-for-profit, where I was told that my triangle theory was bullshit (wasn't the first time I've been told that ...), because they were working without being remunerated. I replied that I didn't say each of the three requirements for keeping staff happy had to be equally weighted (3/9 for remuneration, 3/9 for satisfaction, 3/9 for input). At different stages of your career, each of those three attributes may carry a different weighting. For a person working for free at a not-for-profit, job satisfaction and having input into decision making are clearly far more important than remuneration. However, the person at the presentation obviously didn't need to worry about mortgage repayments or paying private school fees. It's different for everyone, depending on where you are in your life journey – and the ability to recognise that is an important skill for a founder. You have to identify what will get that superstar over the line.

What I do know for sure is that you don't want your employees saying anything like this:

- I love my job, but I can't pay my bills on this salary.

- I hate my job, but I'll keep putting up with this crap until I pay off the mortgage – and then I'm outta here.

- I'm basically told to leave my brain at the front door and pick it up on the way home – nobody values my input.

Your role as a founder is to ensure that your employees are compensated at a market-related salary, love coming to work every day and have a say in what they do. I always say that 99 per cent of the great ideas at Com Tech came from people other than me. Some managers think they just pay for people's arms, legs and backs – without considering that their brains also come as part of the deal.

So, in return for the company delivering on its commitments, what should you expect from an employee?

Firstly, you want your staff to deliver legendary customer service. I've pretty much beaten this topic to death in an earlier chapter, but legendary customer service applies equally to both internal and external customers. There are some people who may never deal with an external customer, but the same rules regarding customer service apply to internal customers – that internal customer is probably relying on some information to support an external customer. A software developer may not be dealing directly with the end customer, but meeting her timeline promptly and reliably will be important to the project manager who is liaising directly with the customer.

Secondly, you only want team players. No one is bigger than the team and the team always comes first. As Reid Hoffman, LinkedIn founder, put it: 'Life is a team sport, not an individual sport. Once you start thinking that way, everything goes a lot better.' You don't want to build a company around brilliant jerks – people who may not be willing to share knowledge or to work well as a team, or who may cause division between different areas of the company.

Finally, you need people who consistently add value. It's not how long they have been with a company or how many hours they work, it's only their contribution that counts. Your best Microsoft engineer may have been a star performer when customers were implementing on-premise solutions, but if that superstar didn't re-engineer their skills to support cloud-based computing then they no longer add value to the company. My former marketing manager,

Merle Singer, once told me that her old boss used to say, 'If you want to know how important you are in a company, punch your hand in a bucket of water – the hole that you leave is the hole that you leave in a company'; i.e., you make no difference. How could I possibly say this when I genuinely believed that in our company, our people were our number one asset? I would often retell Merle's story, but would say, 'I want you to think that you are punching your hand in a bucket of putty, so that you would leave an indelible hole if you were to move from one part of the company to another, one region to another – or worse, leave our company'; i.e., you want to make a massive impact in the role in which you are working.

● ● ●

It's not just about attracting, it's about engaging and retaining, too – it's about continually investing in your number one asset.

CHAPTER 13

Your number one asset is not a number

One of the greatest opportunities that a founder or manager can have is the opportunity to make people in their company feel special.

All too often, people – your number one asset – leave a company because they feel they are just that, a number. I think some founders believe that once they've hired a Head of People or a Chief Happiness Officer (or whatever you want to name the role) it is okay to abrogate their own responsibility for managing people.

This is so wrong. As a founder, you should always be an HR manager – the way you treat people will filter through the organisation. You should still be the number one recruiter, the person who ensures that your culture is maintained and who can motivate people to be the best they can possibly be. Your job is to guarantèe that even as your company grows (and with the right vision and people it will), everybody feels that they are a key component of the team and that their contribution is valued by the company – especially by you!

I want to give you five examples, so that you can better understand how simple this critical role can be.

1. Invictus

I'm not sure how many of you have seen the movie *Invictus*? It really annoys me when people say that the rugby scenes aren't that good. Of course they're not. Matt Damon, who stars in the film as François Pienaar, captain of the Springbok rugby team, had probably never even heard of the sport prior to making the movie. *Invictus* is the story of how Nelson Mandela used rugby, a sport synonymous with the Apartheid regime, to unite a country.

There is a scene in the movie where Mandela's black security contingent ask him when he will be getting rid of the two white Afrikaner men who had been security guards for former president F.W. De Klerk. Mandela responds that he won't be getting rid of them – they will be joining the team. These are men who not long before would have killed Mandela on sight. Later we see the two white guards having a conversation, which goes along the following lines.

One man asks, 'How do you find the new president?'

To which the other replies, 'With the old president [De Klerk], I was invisible. But with the new president [Mandela], he knows that I like English toffee, so whenever he goes to England he buys me a packet.'

So, for £1, Mandela has turned a man who not long before would have killed him in a heartbeat, into someone who will literally put his life on the line for him – simply because that man no longer feels 'invisible'.

2. Ted Lasso

I loved the Apple TV+ series *Ted Lasso* – and if any of you hasn't watched it, I highly recommend that you do. It's not about football (soccer). It's about how a manager who knows nothing about soccer (I can relate to that – I know nothing about technology despite having been in the industry for 40 years) manages the different personalities at a club, to deliver unexpected results.

One episode in particular is a great example. To paraphrase: Ted asks the team's water boy, 'Hey, Nate, can I have one of your famous drinks?'

To which Nate replies, 'What did you call me?'

'I called you Nate, that is your name isn't it?'

'Yes it is, but nobody has ever called me by my name before.'

How simple was it to win over the water boy – just call him by his name and he is on board. Next time you walk into a convenience store, try calling the person behind the counter by their name and see the smile you get. Not rocket science!

If you want to watch a real-life version of *Ted Lasso*, check out *All or Nothing* – a documentary about Arsenal's manager Mikel Arteta – it's a good lesson in people management.

3. The $20 million return on a $20 breakfast

I wasn't sure whether to have 'the best financial return on a crappy breakfast in history' or simply 'the Prickly Puke' as the header to this point. Sean McCreanor, an absolute legend, is the founder (together with Marko Tomic – yes The Power of Two again) of Assignar, a construction technology company. Sean came to pitch Assignar to OIF Ventures a few years ago, saying, 'I only want to partner with OIF Ventures because I used to work with Dave at Com Tech and I will never forget my first day at work – he took me for breakfast. I know how he values people.' The local cafe (which was named after a type of cactus) was so bad we affectionately renamed it the Prickly Puke. So it wasn't the quality of the meal, it was the quality of the time that I, as the founder, was willing to spend with our number one asset – people. We recently sold 50 per cent of our investment in

Assignar, for $10 million. We invested $4 million, and hopefully in addition to the $10 million already returned there will still be a big chunk of cash to follow. Not a bad return for a $20 breakfast.

I presented to a bunch of founders not that long ago, and one of them said, 'Dave, now that we've grown, I don't even know some of my team members' names.'

'How many people do you have, Rick?'

'Thirty.'

'Mate, that's bullshit. Thirty is nothing. Your homework is that by next week you will have taken every member of your team who you have yet to meet, for breakfast, coffee, lunch or dinner.'

Getting to know your team is not that hard – and today, with flexible work and work-from-home options, it is more important than ever.

4. Does he drink with us?

One of the best people I ever had the privilege of working with is Melpo Pupulas. Melpo joined us as sales support (customer success) from our competitor, Merisel, a large US-listed company.

I will never forget having drinks with the team one night and overhearing Melpo saying to another team member, 'Does he [being me] drink with the staff?' I thought to myself, how lucky am I – we have just hired one of Merisel's most valuable people, and the best part is that their CEO doesn't even realise their loss, just because they were too important to drink with everyone in the company. I've been trying to headhunt Melps for years, but just can't get her out of retirement!

5. Dom, what a CHAMP

When I was acting CEO of Centric Wealth, I spent quite a bit of time at CHAMP, the private equity firm that owned 80 per cent of the company. I always used to chat to the lady on reception, Dom. I once asked her how long she had been with CHAMP, to which she replied, 'Twelve years.' She told me she loved her job, and when I asked why, she said, 'Every Friday, Bill [Bill Ferris, in addition to being an absolute legend, was the founder of CHAMP and is affectionately referred to as the father of private equity in Australia] would ask me what the plans for the weekend were, and on Monday he would ask how the weekend went.' It wasn't because CHAMP paid her a bucketload of cash or gave her eight weeks leave, it was simply because Bill, the founder, genuinely cared about Dom as a human being.

● ● ●

As a founder, you should always be an HR manager – you should always be recruiting. The way you treat people will filter through the organisation.

CHAPTER 14

Advice from the best

Early in my career, while I was on a flight from Sydney to the USA, I happened to be reading the latest edition of *Fortune* magazine.

In that magazine was a summary of a book called *Control Your Destiny or Someone Else Will*. The book was about Jack Welch, the legendary CEO of GE.

Jack had six rules for success, which actually formed the basis for my own management style. These rules are not just useful business lessons – they can easily be translated into life lessons as well.

1. Face reality as it is, not as it was or you wish it to be.

2. Change before you have to.

3. Don't manage, lead.

4. If you don't have a competitive advantage, don't compete.

5. Be candid with everyone.

6. Control your destiny or someone else will.

I still believe that a leader who can consistently execute on ALL of these six rules will be well positioned to build a long-term, sustainable company. It's amazing how visionary and relevant these rules were – and still are. Consider the first two. The current way of expressing these concepts is that if you don't want to be disrupted, you better pivot – or you will become irrelevant. Disrupt or be disrupted! If you don't face reality when things around you are changing (no matter how hard that may be), if you don't pivot, then you will become irrelevant and disappear. So many successful companies have fallen into this trap.

Face reality as it is, not as it was or you wish it to be

Complacency, and the desire to protect a highly profitable revenue stream, are the biggest challenges that an incumbent will face. So many companies have been killed simply because they didn't want the status quo to change. It has become very relevant for a founder today as the capital markets have changed.

I sat on the board of Fairfax between 1999 and 2002. Fairfax was for many years a highly successful media company. They had a monopoly on the information that underpins the three major life decisions (aside from marriage) that people make: where we are going to work, which house we should buy and what car we want to drive. So lucrative were these revenues, derived from their major mastheads – *The Sydney Morning Herald*, *The Age* and the *Financial Review* – that they were known as 'The Rivers of Gold'. Why would Fairfax want this to change? Only an exceptional manager would have recognised that the internet was about to disrupt their core business AND been willing to embrace the opportunity that it presented – even though, in the short term, it may have had an impact on Fairfax's Rivers of Gold. I don't think Fairfax saw either the threat or the opportunity presented by the internet. To me, it was completely obvious that classified advertising was so well suited to the Net – sorting lots of information by price, by neighbourhood, by job, etc. But when you had hundreds of millions of dollars of revenue to protect, only a bold leader would have said: 'If somebody is going to kill our core business, it's going to be us.'

As I've stated before, in business you need a few lucky breaks – and for SEEK, realestate.com.au (REA) and carsales.com.au, Fairfax was theirs. By the early part of the 2000s, Fairfax had become irrelevant, and by 2018 it had disappeared, swallowed up by Nine Entertainment for about $3 billion. The combined market capitalisations of the three disruptors is about $40 billion. Fairfax didn't want to face reality as it was, so it continued to wish that things would stay just as they had been during those glory years. The only consolation for Fairfax is that there are so many other Fairfaxes out there: Barnes and Noble got Amazoned, Netflix killed Blockbuster and Uber challenged the taxi industry. So, as a founder, if you don't want your Kodak moment, face reality as it is, not as it was or as you wish it to be.

Not all startups succeed. In fact, most fail, despite the best endeavours of hard-working founders. Sometimes what may have seemed like the best idea on a PowerPoint slide presentation may not end up being that easy to execute. My advice: if, after a reasonable period of time, you know it's not going to happen, face reality as it is, not as you wish it to be. Move on! I have worked with founders who never want to say die. They fall in love with their idea and don't know when to surrender. I have seen this cost founders so much in their future careers – they just went on too long.

Change before you have to

In some respects, it is easy to change when your core business is bleeding. But the challenge for any founder is to change while your core business is *strong*. Intel, the world's dominant microprocessor supplier, only got into microprocessors because their core business, memory chips, had in fact become just that – a memory.

Intel had no choice but to pivot. The Japanese suppliers Fujitsu and Toshiba had crushed them. If Intel hadn't changed, the company may have disappeared. Under the leadership of industry icon Andy Grove, they pivoted to become a microprocessor company – and, as they say, the rest is history. By contrast, pivoting when your core business is on the *decline* doesn't usually have a happy ending. Kodak tried to embrace digital technology when their core print business was nearly dead, Fairfax tried to embrace the internet when it was way too late, and the giants of retail in the USA are no longer giants.

As a founder, you have to constantly be thinking, *What and who could kill my company?* Complacency kills successful companies. The iPhone came about because Steve Jobs asked that exact question: *What could kill the iPod?* While still generating massive cash flows from the iPod, Apple pivoted. Recognising what the phone had done to the camera, Steve Jobs wasn't going to let that happen to the music player. So, yes, Steve Jobs – marketing genius. But just as importantly, Steve Jobs – business genius, too. While Apple's core business (excuse the pun) was thriving, he pivoted and made it the most valuable company in the world. It would have been so much harder if he had waited for a phone company to incorporate an MP3 player into a phone. Who uses the iPod today? Nobody, it's embedded in the smartphone – in most cases, fortunately, in the Apple iPhone.

But did the same company that revolutionised the music industry by disrupting the record/CD industry become disrupted itself? Perhaps! The industry has evolved from records, to CDs, to Apple's download service, to music streaming – now led by a new player, Spotify. Although Apple changed before they had to in order to protect the revenue streams from the iPod, they didn't evolve as the industry evolved to streaming, and they are now playing catchup to keep pace with market leader Spotify.

Don't manage, lead

I remember one of my team once saying to me, 'Dave, I really respect you.' I asked him why, and he said, 'Because you're the CEO of Com Tech.' I replied: 'Jase, if that's the only reason why you respect me, I'm not that flattered – any idiot can register a company for $900 and call themselves CEO, founder, president or whatever the hell they want. If you respect me because I have articulated a clear vision for the company, we are executing on that vision and I treat people with respect no matter where they work, *then* I'm flattered. But not if I'm respected for having a bloody title on a business card.' More about leadership in a later chapter.

If you don't have a competitive advantage, don't compete

At the beginning of this book, I said that being a founder is not easy. So, if you're going to have a crack, make sure that you give yourself the best chance of winning. I was fortunate enough to get into local area networking just as it was about to take off. The incumbent had gotten fat and lazy, and had no regard for customer service. There was a massive opportunity to dominate the market for this rapidly growing industry in Australia.

Together with a small team, we seized the opportunity and executed. We had 70 per cent of the networking market in Australia. It was growing at 40 per cent per annum. Six months after I had been appointed as a Novell distributor, Novell added another two distributors. Com Tech never relinquished our market share and position – we continued to grow while the others floundered. Our timing was impeccable: the incumbent was ripe to be disrupted and the two new players had a formidable competitor in Com Tech. They never had a chance.

As a founder, always make sure that your timing is right – it's probably the most important indicator of future success. Imagine trying to compete with Canva today. They were first to market and executed flawlessly, and they now have a dominant position in the global market in a category that they have created: a graphic design platform category. It will be very hard to break their dominant position, and it would be foolish for a new entrant with no competitive advantage to try and enter the market. If you can't beat 'em, find another idea – you don't want to make your startup harder than it's going to be anyway.

Be candid with everyone

I always tell my boys that if they only learn one thing from me, it should be, 'My word is my bond.' It's the best advice that I can give any founder. You don't *deserve* respect, you *earn* it – from your employees, your customers, your business partners and your shareholders. The best way to lose respect is when your actions don't match your words. Once you have made a commitment, always honour it, even if you may have screwed up. Perhaps you promised a bonus to someone who subsequently hasn't earned it – you still need to pay it!

Being honest with everyone means telling people the truth, not just what they want to hear. If you know a staff member is not meeting their objectives, let them know that if things don't change it may be best that they get their CV up to date. It is better than telling them how great they are today and getting HR to fire them tomorrow. If you're having customer service issues and you don't share those issues with people in the front line, how do you fix those problems? I was always extremely transparent with our team and shared all news – good and bad. That's how we solved problems together. If I look back on my career, I really think that my candid and empathetic management style was the main reason I earned the respect of the constituents that are key to any business: staff, customers, business partners and shareholders.

I always appreciated business partners who were open and honest with us. Gary Jackson, the country manager for Cisco, told me, 'Don't waste your time selling to the big four banks and the telcos, we do that business direct.' I knew not to waste our valuable resources bidding on these opportunities when I would only lose to the vendor. We focused on what we *could* win, and there was still more than enough for us to build a great business around Cisco. If I valued Gary's honesty, I knew that anyone dealing with me would feel the same.

Control your destiny or someone else will

You control your own destiny when you have a highly motivated, energised and aligned team of people all working towards the same goal. As a founder, attracting and retaining a team of great people, and motivating them to be the best that they can possibly be, is one of your key functions. Culture flows from the top down. Companies, no matter what size, are capable of anything when you have a highly motivated team.

In 1996, nine years after we had started, Com Tech had 240 people. We were doing $165 million in revenue and making a profit of $14 million – on paper, it seemed like an amazing business. However, I saw storm clouds ahead. Our two major vendors, Novell and Bay Networks, were floundering, while Microsoft and Cisco were thriving. The industry was growing, so the fact that our two major vendors were shrinking was therefore not an industry problem. Clearly, we had the wrong products in our portfolio. If we didn't sign up with the two market leaders, Cisco and Microsoft, then, like our incumbent vendors Novell and Bay Networks, we too would become irrelevant.

Our company strategy for our first nine years of existence was: *We sell the number one OR number two product in the market.* It worked really well when our major vendors commanded 70 per cent market share, but when that changed, I knew that I needed to do something different. I changed one word. 'OR' became 'AND'. *We sell the number one AND number two product in the market.* We signed Microsoft and Cisco, in addition to selling Novell and Bay Networks.

We made other major changes to our business too. In addition to being a distribution company and a training company, we became a systems integration company in Australia, serving the ASX 200. We also rebranded our distribution business to Express Data. To effect these changes, we needed the support of about 100 of our staff – that was 40 per cent of our entire company. Not a word got out to the industry.

Without an unbelievable team, we could never have achieved what we did. Within a year, we had grown to over 1000 people and were market leaders in the three areas that we addressed: technical training, the distribution of networking and communication products, and our new line of business – network integration. It was hard work, but I'm always grateful to the amazing team we had in place who allowed us to control our own destiny before someone else did.

● ● ●

CHAPTER 15

The 1 per cent factor

When someone knows 1 per cent more than you, they seem like a genius. Beware, this misconception could be fatal.

When I started Com Tech, I had no funding and no technical capability. Through my initial job in Australia, I had met these two accountants who professed to be networking experts. So, when I went out on my own, they offered me a shared desk (maybe that was the forerunner to WeWork) and said they would serve as my tech team when I needed to provide tech support to my customers. I literally shared a desk, and my phone number was their third number on a rotary phone system: 29 6196. If they were using all three lines, Com Tech was literally uncontactable. In 1987, mobile phones and email weren't pervasive and very few companies had fax machines – but hey, that was the best that I could afford.

When customers started asking tech questions, I very quickly realised that someone who may have seemed like a tech expert to a novice/tech Luddite was in fact nothing more than an accountant with extremely limited technical knowledge.

If the dentist tells you that you need root canal treatment, you trust them because they are perceived experts in their field. You would assume that after six years at uni and on-the-job training they *should* be. Imagine if they weren't. You're not relying on someone simply because they know 1 per cent more than you. Relying on someone in your company who portrays themselves as an expert, but is not, is like putting your company through root canal treatment without an anaesthetic. Make sure that, like your dentist, the person you are relying on in a particular area where you lack the expertise is truly an expert in their field and not just someone who knows slightly more than you do.

Four months after starting Com Tech, I realised something had to change. My weakness was on the tech side and I desperately needed my own in-house technical capability. I couldn't rely on people who knew 1 per cent more than I did – effectively, they knew nothing.

I decided that I really needed to get my own office with my own dedicated team. I happened to mention to one of my wife's friends that I was looking for a tech expert and she said, 'I know this guy, he is a genius.' She made the introduction to the first person I ever hired – after myself – Nathan Cher, and he sure is a genius, probably the smartest person I have ever met. I would love to say that it happened because of my brilliant recruiting skills, but in reality it was another one of those lucky breaks.

Nathan had come from a minicomputer (Digital Equipment Corp – DEC) multi-user environment, while most of our customers had only worked in a stand-alone PC environment. The Novell documentation, which comprised a huge collection of manuals, literally looked like *Encyclopaedia Britannica* (you will probably have to go to Wikipedia to find out what that was). After his first day at work, Nathan said, 'This is pretty easy.' I looked at him, dumbfounded, and he explained that it was very similar to what he had been doing – only the syntax was different. The next day, he took his first support call. Sure enough, he delivered amazing customer service and I knew that I had hit the jackpot. Nathan truly was a technical expert, and from the day that he joined I never, ever worried about the tech side of the business again. My next hire was a friend of mine, Dan Jarzin, to whom I have dedicated this book. I hired Dan to look after all the accounting and back office requirements. After two months, Dan's wife told him to get a job with a reputable company and he moved on (only to return about seven years later, when we were more established), and in his place I hired my brother, Jon. Because Dan was initially only with us for a few weeks, I always think of both him and Jon as my 'third hire'. Being extremely vulnerable regarding tech, my fourth, fifth, sixth and seventh hires were all tech – I wanted to make sure that if Nathan left, I was well covered.

Darron Lonstein was the fourth hire. He came to us on the recommendation of another of my wife's friends – I told you that your life partner is key, even if they don't work in the business. Darron was also brilliant, more reserved than Nathan but equally smart. He too had come from a multi-user (Unix) environment and he picked up Novell just as quickly. Natie and Daz were superstars, and I appointed them both directors and shareholders in the company. I think it was a win/win outcome for all of us. Nathan and Darron were phenomenal as a team – as I've said before, the Power of Two really works. Nathan was probably the best technical presenter in the IT industry. With his golden tonsils and his technical prowess, he had the ability to captivate an audience – from salespeople to CTOs – irrespective of their capability. Darron was the better people manager. He literally led by example, and when the shit hit the fan, which it often does when implementing new technology solutions, it wasn't uncommon to find Darron working all-nighters with his team. He commanded such respect from his team: not because of a title on his business card, but because he was hugely knowledgeable and knew how to roll up his sleeves when his team needed help.

Nathan and Darron hired arguably the best technical team in the country, many of whom have gone on to command senior roles at banks and telcos and to become company founders. I'm so proud of what our technical guys have achieved. It was our technical-led expertise that resulted in our dominant market position in every area in which we competed.

Many years later, I met a guy who told me that he was going to build the next Com Tech. I wished him good luck and asked him what his tech team was like. He replied, 'Excellent.' I asked how he knew, and he said because he had personally hired them. Like me, Adam was an accountant. I said that if I could get Darron to interview his team, I would be able to tell him if he was going to build the next Com Tech. If Darron thought they were good, then he had a shot – you can't add value to your customers in a network integration company if you don't have a highly competent technical team. After he conducted the interviews, an embarrassed Darron came back and said, 'Dave, I wouldn't hire one of them.' To Adam, they were experts because they knew 1 per cent more than he did. To a real expert, they were incompetent. And that was why Adam hadn't succeeded yet. To his credit, he replaced his entire team and then went on to build a successful managed-services company, which he later sold in a life-changing transaction. I was honoured to have mentored him.

The moral of the story is that, whenever possible, you should use experts to help you hire people in those areas where you have limited capability. Nobody can be good at everything, and you don't want to be blindsided by the 1 per cent factor. How would you know a good customer success person if you have never worked in that role or hired a customer success person?

Importantly, I should also say that although I always relied on Nathan and Darron to confirm the technical capability of a potential employee, I generally interviewed the candidate myself to ensure that anyone we hired was culturally aligned to our business values. We only wanted people who had both the attitude and ability to work at Com Tech – just one of these attributes was not enough.

● ● ●

I couldn't rely on people who knew 1 per cent more than I did – effectively they knew nothing.

CHAPTER 16

To raise, or not to raise?

The million-dollar question: to raise, or not to raise?

If you can run your startup without external funding, that's definitely the best option. But in most cases, especially when you are still investing in R&D, building your brand and sales capability, this is not possible. If you can't continue to self-fund your startup, then you are going to need to find an investor. I can't emphasise enough: it's not just about the money – once you take the cash, you are joined at the hip. The key is finding an investor who will give you the cash at a fair valuation AND bring some value add to your company. They all say they do, but I suggest that you call as many of their portfolio companies as possible and make sure that their actions match their words. You don't want to screw up this important decision. When I decided to take in a private equity partner, I worked with Michael Traill from Macquarie Bank. My logic being that if I were to go out with Mike and his wife Jenny for dinner, it was not because I had to, it was because I wanted to. That was in 1992, and 30 years later I'm still mates with Trailly. Of course, I wanted a fair valuation – but I would rather have taken a lower, but reasonable, valuation to work with Mike than a higher valuation to work with someone who was not culturally aligned with Com Tech. It turned out to be an excellent decision for both Mac Bank and Com Tech.

A VC partnership is like a marriage. You don't take a chance with what may appear to be the best option – the highest valuation – unless there is great chemistry. You must be working as a team, not as adversaries. Even though you may not be working with each other day to day, choosing a VC partner is almost like selecting a co-founder. Try and find a partner who will not only write a cheque but will also bring complementary skills. If you are a tech founder, then a sales and marketing oriented partner may be a good fit.

The next key decision is how much you should raise. Founders often suffer from what I refer to as 'founders' euphoria'. They believe that because they love their idea – and you must, as a founder, or nobody will – everybody else will love it too and customers will be salivating to get their hands on the product or service. Unfortunately, it doesn't usually work like that. Remember, it always takes longer and costs more than you think. I always advise founders that they can't afford to be reckless in either direction regarding capital raising. Don't take on too much capital and don't take on too little. Make sure that you have enough runway to give yourself the best opportunity to execute on your business plan – and to enable you to get to the next raise, an exit or ideally a long-term sustainable business that is profitable and cash-flow positive (see chapter 5 to recall what constitutes a long-term sustainable business). But don't take on too much, or you could end up so diluted that you may not own your idea at the next raise.

To help provide a clearer explanation, I thought it would be useful to give a couple of examples based on VC investments that I've been involved with.

One of our best founders raised $2 million for a Series A to execute on his business plan. He told me that he was going to hire ten salespeople with the funding. I advised him that if he did that, it wouldn't be long before he would be laying off eight non-performing salespeople and coming back to us for more capital – and then we would own his business. I didn't want that. We back founders and we want them to be heavily incentivised for us to succeed – we are not looking to back salaried managers with limited equity. For the stage his business was at, there was nobody better suited than the sales-orientated founder to win those key anchor tenants, making it much easier for the second, third and fourth salespeople to come on board and reference those happy customers. Enterprise selling is a body contact sport. I needed that founder pounding the streets to win those first few customers. He later told me that this was the best advice he ever got. In two years, he has grown his revenues from $250,000 of annual recurring revenue (ARR) to over $15 million of ARR; he still owns 45 per cent of his company, and those original customers that he closed helped him to build his business. Using $2 million to build a sales team at that early stage would have been a reckless decision.

Recently, we met some awesome tech founders who had built an amazing product that was quickly getting traction across the globe with incredible customers. They had bootstrapped the company with their own funds and were now faced with the following choices:

- Continue to bootstrap.
- Do a smaller raise in Australia.
- Do a big US raise.

We were really keen to invest in the startup, but I wanted to give them candid advice, whether they went with us or not. It's the only way to operate.

I advised the founders that doing nothing would be conservatively reckless. They had a great opportunity in front of them, and if they failed to seek extra funding they would not be giving their startup the best chance to build the market-leading solution for the problem they were solving. Some of their customers were asking them to raise funding so they could continue to invest in adding new features and functionality to their product. They needed to raise cash!

As they were tech founders, I suggested that they take on an Australian-based VC company for their Series A (hopefully us), to help them build the systems and infrastructure they would need to eventually expand offshore. Their next raise should be in the USA – but not this one. Taking a large US round at this early stage would have been reckless too. Going from bootstrapping, to having millions of dollars in the bank to spend, requires a completely different mindset. And why would you want a partner 15,000 kilometres away at this critical time for the business?

It's a fine balance, calculating how much runway you'll need in order to execute, how much dilution you can stomach and which VC partnership is the right one for your startup. It's going to be one of the most important decisions that you will make in your early career as a founder – consider it wisely.

● ● ●

CHAPTER 17

Do I have an option about granting share options?

I'm super proud that Com Tech was an early initiator of giving our key staff options as part of their package.

Not many companies had a share option plan for their staff in 1990. I remember saying to my brother, Steven, 'How good would you feel if one day Peta Rothpletz [an extraordinary member of our admin team] was able to say, *I paid off my house because of the difference that I made at Com Tech?*'

I remember calling my lawyer and telling him that I wanted to set up an appointment so that we could put in place a share incentive plan for our staff. When we met, he spent an hour telling me about all the complexities involved and why I shouldn't do this. I told him that if I wanted to know how hard it was, I wouldn't have called him – I called because I wanted a share plan set up. I called another lawyer, my now business partner Geoff Levy, who put in place a share incentive plan that proved to be mutually beneficial for both Com Tech and our team. Today, share option plans are far more pervasive, and most law firms would understand both the importance and mechanics of setting up a plan.

We allocated 15 per cent of our equity to management and staff. I have never looked back and said *boy, I wish I hadn't allocated so much*. I have always been a huge supporter of 'better to have a smaller share of a bigger pie', and that's exactly what happened. I do not believe that we would have achieved what we did without a highly energised, aligned team of people. I'm not suggesting that staff owning a small piece of the company leads to alignment or engagement – remember, remuneration, of which share options are one tool, is only a part of what keeps staff happy. Job satisfaction, company culture and having the opportunity to contribute to the direction of the company are equally as important. I would hate to have people working in my company just because they were sitting on lucrative stock options and were merely waiting for those options to vest before they moved on.

One of the best parts of being a founder, in addition to that big exit, is seeing people who have helped you get there achieve way more than they dreamed possible, both professionally and financially. I can say that when I look back on my career, the thing that I'm most proud of is that we were able to change the lives of so many people – a fair return for someone who was willing to back a young founder with no experience but just a dream to build an amazing tech company. Oh, yes – Peta Rothpletz did pay off her mortgage, thanks to the initiative of ensuring that our staff shared in the success of the company.

Often I get asked, 'how much should I allocate to our executive staff option plan [ESOP], and should I give all our staff options?' I don't have all the answers and it's not a matter of one size fits all. What worked for me was giving fewer staff a meaningful allocation of options, as opposed to giving anyone who joined the company share options. Options were given to those people who went above and beyond, people who fitted in the top right quadrant and met objectives and shared the values of the company. These were people who we never wanted to see leave the company. We also didn't allocate everyone the exact same number of options – not everyone is created equal. The quantum was determined by the importance of the role, the seniority of the individual and the cultural fit of the staff member.

Generally, most companies will allocate about 10 per cent of the shares of the company in ESOP, and allocate this over a period of time. Often on the next capital raise the ESOP is topped back up to 10 per cent, to ensure your company can continue to attract and retain key people.

So, to conclude, you do have an option about granting share options – but to me, allowing those staff who make a massive difference to your company the ability to share in the success of the company is a no-brainer. Not only will it help you succeed on your own journey, but it will also provide you with immense satisfaction when you realise how many lives you've been able to change as you collectively turn that dream into a reality.

● ● ●

We were able
to change the
lives of so many
people, thanks
to the initiative
of ensuring our
staff shared in
the success of the
company.

CHAPTER 18

Do you have a board of directors or are you bored of directors?

Another important decision for a founder is who will sit on your board.

Your choice of directors and/or mentors is crucial. These are the people you may want to turn to when the going gets tough. Do they have both the experience and commitment to support you when you need it most? Commitment, trust, relationship quality and director/mentor competence are the real ingredients required to support a founder's developmental growth.

I have already shared my views on sitting on a public company board – it's clearly not for me, as I could never see the value that I could add when I was so far removed from the day to day. Once again, this is only my view. There are many successful board members who have made a massive difference to the management teams and shareholders they serve – I'm just not one of them. To me, the most important decision that a public company board can make is choosing the right CEO. In my opinion, once they have done this, their role – aside from involvement in the normal governance and regulatory matters – is to ensure that they have provided the CEO and the management team with all the resources they require to execute on the strategy that the CEO and leadership team have defined.

To my mind, formulating strategy is *not* part of the board's role. If the board has to set the strategy, then clearly you have the wrong CEO. The board should be a sounding board, helping to validate the executive leadership team's strategy and providing input where past experience may provide some valuable insight.

As a partner in OIF Ventures, I sincerely believe that our biggest challenge is picking the right founder, as opposed to picking the best idea. Once you have identified an exceptional founder, you then evaluate both the idea and the size of the opportunity – and whether or not it is worth deploying capital into that opportunity. The right idea with the wrong founder will generally lead to a subpar return. How do I know that? I've made this mistake myself!

Once you have made the decision to back a founder, you are often given the opportunity to appoint a director to the company. From a founder's perspective, as always, you want a director with whom you are culturally aligned. Bob Mansfield (former McDonald's Australia CEO), Bob Dwyer (former coach of the national Australian rugby union team), Ian Chappell (former Australian cricket captain) and Michael Traill (Macquarie Bank) were all external directors of Com Tech. They were not there because of their status. I am still mates with all of them today because we were and still are culturally aligned, and because they brought complementary and diverse skills to our board. Bob Mansfield was my chairman and mentor and we remain both friends and business partners today – Bob is an investor in OIF's VC fund. I tease him that I'm still making money for him 25 years after we first met.

The reason our board worked was that we all knew each other's strengths and weaknesses. Nobody was expected, nor is anyone expected, to know everything. The fact that Bob had been CEO of McDonald's and then first CEO of Optus (Australia's second telecommunications carrier) didn't mean that he knew everything. Like me, Bob was extremely customer- and staff-focused, and that's why I chose him as my chairperson. We thought very similarly. However, Bob had run companies way larger than Com Tech, and I believed I could learn how to scale without compromising on our levels of staff and customer satisfaction – so important to our success. Sometimes, the close working relationship between the founder and the chairperson/mentor means it may only be the founder who recognises the value of that chairperson or mentor. In my case, as a founder I was always aware that the buck stopped with me. If Com Tech failed, it wasn't going to be Steve or Jon Shein who had failed, it was going to be *David* Shein.

I must admit, I did fear failure. It was nice to know that I always had Bob in my corner, and while I can't say that he came up with any part of our strategy, he was always there as a sounding board – someone to bounce ideas off and, importantly, to share my challenges with. When Com Tech eventually sold to DiData, they said the fact we could attract someone like Bob to our board gave them even more confidence that we were the right partner to lead their Asia–Pacific growth plans.

There is a huge difference between private equity and venture capital. I have seen private equity companies attempt to move into the VC space without recognising the difference. In private equity, you want to be the major shareholder, looking in some cases to replace the CEO, make acquisitions, cut costs and position the business for sale in a few years time.

With venture capital, you are generally a minority shareholder, and you want the founder and leadership team to own the majority of the capital – especially in the early stages. 'What share of the company do you own?' is one of the first questions we ask a founder. If it's not enough, we don't invest. We back founders, not managers. With venture capital – while you should always be conscious of the burn rate and how much runway a company has to get to their next stage of growth – the role is to grow the business, not cut costs.

Regarding appointing directors, I'm going to discuss what I know: venture capital. To me, the role of a director is to support a founder in whatever way they can – it's important to recognise that this could be a founder's first gig and that they may not have all the required skills. I know that I didn't have them when I founded Com Tech (and I still don't have all the skills today). This is the opportunity for you to make a difference and really add value. Can you help the founder attract staff to fill any gaps they may have in their company or find the anchor tenant that could be a company-changing opportunity? Can you assist with back-office tasks such as accounting, legal and HR until they have the resources to implement these services in house? We see an OIF VC director's role as giving the founder whatever support they need so that they can focus on what they are good at, without ever forgetting that the founder is the CEO. At OIF Ventures we ask ourselves every day: what value (aside from a cheque) have we added to our portfolio companies today? What difference did we make to a company? What did we contribute to each investment that helped them succeed? Would it have been possible for them to achieve the same outcome without our involvement?

What is key here is that the board's role is not to run the company – its role is to support the founder/s and the leadership team. If you, the board, are running the company, you should not have backed the founder. The founder/board relationship is not a manager/ employee relationship, it's a team effort where both parties are working towards delivering the best outcome to the founders, staff and investors. It's that simple. So, my advice is for a founder to find like-minded people who bring diverse skills to an organisation. A tech founder appointing a sales-orientated director makes a lot of sense, and vice versa.

● ● ●

A board's role is to support, challenge and validate a strategy, not set it. The CEO and leadership team should be responsible for setting and implementing the strategy. If the board sets the strategy, you have backed the wrong founder.

CHAPTER 19

The world is my oyster

Atlassian is Atlassian because its flagship product, Jira, is the industry-standard, market-leading product globally.

Jira dominates the market in the USA, the UK and Germany – and, consequently, in Australia. When (like Jira) your product solves a generic problem, you have no choice but to be a global player.

Whether we like it or not, Australia only represents approximately 2 per cent of the global market, while the USA represents about 50 per cent of the world market for technology products and services. In order to win, you have to win in the USA – and then the rest of the world, maybe with the exception of China, will fall like dominoes. Every product that is the market leader in the USA is generally the market leader in Singapore, France,

Brazil and Australia. So, if the problem that your product or service solves is generic, it's no good just being the King or Queen of Australia. From the outset, you need to be thinking about how you're going to conquer the world.

Let's assume that the total addressable market (TAM) for your product category is $100 million. Say that your startup, OziSoftware, wins the entire Australian market. Your total sales will be about $2 million. In the meantime, your US competitor, YankeeSoft, is generating $50 million in sales. You put 40 per cent of your revenues into R&D, and YankeeSoft put 20 per cent of theirs into R&D. You're spending $800,000 compared with YankeeSoft's $10 million. No matter how good your engineers are, you're going to lose. YankeeSoft will out-innovate you, out-market you and out-sell you and soon your home market will be gone. They will be in the Gartner Magic Quadrant and selling to the *Fortune* 500. The more customers, the more validation, the better the roadmap and the easier it will be to sell.

Australia is a great base in which to build software. Our engineers are as good as any in the world. And we have some customers that are large enough to help provide a critical level of initial validation and vital feedback. If your product is good enough for a big Australian bank, it will be good enough for a big US bank; if you're good enough for Telstra, you will be good enough for Sprint.

Having said that, some products or services *can* succeed by specifically addressing the Australian market. MYOB built a great company just by selling accounting software in Australia (although they did have a shot at overseas expansion), and companies like SEEK, realestate.com and carsales.com could easily have built extremely successful companies just operating in Australia – although, for growth, they have all pursued global opportunities. But the great Australian software success stories, like Atlassian, Canva, WiseTech, Appen, Aconex, CultureAmp and Safety Culture (and the many others that will follow), could never have achieved what they have, just by selling into a market that represents only 2 per cent of the total addressable market. It's simply a numbers game.

How do I know all this? Because, unfortunately, I am writing with experience on my side. After I left Com Tech, I mentored the founder of an awesome company called Holly. I actually became the executive chairman and I learnt a lot about adding value to a founder and CEO in this capacity – it defined my future career. If you were to look at the pitch deck for Holly today, you would think it must be the business plan for Siri or Alexa. Holly was a speech-recognition

To succeed as an Australian startup, you need the USA to succeed from a sales and market-share perspective.

To do this, you will need Australia to deliver from an R&D perspective. Therefore both the USA and Australia will be critical to your success. Atlassian is Atlassian because they dominate the USA from a market-share perspective – and once you win the USA, the rest of the world (with the exception of China) generally follows.

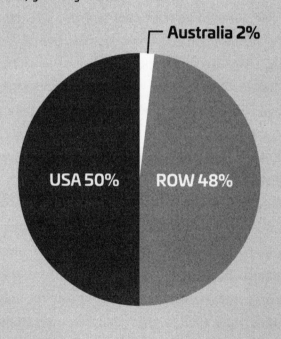

Australia 2%

USA 50%   ROW 48%

platform. *Holly, what will the weather be like tomorrow? Holly, what is the stock price of Apple?* Nothing mind-blowing today, but this was in 2000. We were going to be the world's first voice-search portal. After the dot-com crash, we had to pivot the business to become a software-based interactive voice response (IVR) platform. We started winning some great accounts in Australia: all three Australian telcos, Telstra, Optus and Vodafone, became referenceable customers and they still use Holly today.

Unfortunately, the Holly of the USA was a company called VoiceGenie. They were winning big in the United States while we were winning in Australia. The USA is 13 times larger than Australia in terms of population size, so VoiceGenie were generating far more sales and winning far more customers than we were. We waited too long to launch there and we paid the price. When we did enter the USA, it was almost impossible to displace VoiceGenie, even with a far superior product. We eventually exited to one of our customers in the USA – West Interactive.

I was really proud of what we achieved at Holly. When I arrived, the culture was toxic – the two founders were killing each other, the software didn't work and we were running out of cash. When we sold, we had one of the best teams that I have ever been privileged to work with (I had fired one of the founders), we were making money, and the software was being used by some of the world's largest telcos. My big regret is that we didn't move fast enough to execute in the USA. It was an expensive lesson to learn – Holly could have dominated the market, had we been bold enough to move more quickly. We were selling a generic software-based IVR platform, and VoiceGenie beat us to it. We missed the boat and were unable to maximise the potential of the opportunity.

While Australia may only represent 2 per cent of sales, it will probably represent 100 per cent of your R&D, at least initially – so it's crucial to have strong leadership in Australia, especially if the founder relocates. Your startup needs Australia to be strong in order for the USA to be strong, while the USA needs to be strong for Australia to be strong. That is, the USA needs to sell lots of product in order to win the lion's share of the 50 per cent of the total addressable market, while Australia needs to deliver, innovate and build a reliable product. Get that right and you could just be the next great company to emerge from Australia.

● ● ●

If the problem that your product solves is generic, it's no good just being the King or Queen of Australia. From the outset, you need to be thinking about how you're going to conquer the world.

CHAPTER 20

To grow, you gotta let go

Probably my smartest realisation when I founded my own company was that there were some things that I would *never, ever* be able to do (technical), and some things that I *could* do – but didn't *want* to do (financials).

I wanted to focus on sales and marketing. And I could only do that once I had surrounded myself with people who were far more capable than I was when it came to those things that I couldn't do – and those things that I simply didn't want to do. Once I had hired people in those key positions, I was deeply grateful that I never, ever had to worry about the tech or financial side of the company again. Sure, I was there when I was needed, but I never interfered in the day-to-day management and nor did I want to.

Some founders love to micromanage. I was the opposite. Once I'd hired the right person for a role, they were empowered to do what they came on board to do and that's how we grew. To grow, you have to let go. It's a matter of being able to trust your team. By trust, I don't mean worrying about someone putting their hand in the cookie jar (that's a given). I mean you trust that person to do the role better than you could do it yourself.

I remember the time I got a really good lesson on how to manage. I held a management meeting for every one of the managers in the company, and on this particular day the guy who ran my Canberra office said: 'Dave, sometimes I ring you to ask for your advice and you say, "Seb, it's your office, make a call."' He told me that 99 out of 100 times he *was* making the call. It was that one time when he did ring me for advice that he really needed my input and support.

This was one of the best lessons I ever got. I'd been so proud of myself, thinking I was empowering people to run their part of the company – yet here was a manager telling me that I wasn't there when he needed me most. It was a defining moment for me as a manager. If a manager needs your help to make 99 out of 100 decisions, then you have the wrong manager for that role. But when you seldom get a phone call and the manager is making great decisions, always make sure that you are there when they do put up their hand asking for your input.

Nobody can possibly be good at everything, nor is it possible to fulfil all the roles required in a fast-growing company yourself. You may be the sole founder, like I was – but to grow, you have to surround yourself with a team of people with a complementary skill set AND like-minded values. Get that right, and you are on your way.

So, what should you be looking for when making these key recruitment decisions? It took me some time to identify what I expected from a person who would be assuming a management position – a role that I was effectively outsourcing to another member of my team. Ultimately, a frustrating situation involving one of my managers made me realise that it boiled down to three key attributes (and all three were required – just having two of them would not be good enough):

1. Vision
2. Hands-on attitude
3. HR skills

Vision

As the founder, you must have the overall vision for where you want the company to be, but you should not be expected to have a vision for every single part of the company.

If you're a tech-led founder, you may know that cash flow, montly recurring revenue (MRR), annual recurring revenue (ARR), pipeline management, expenses, payroll, lease agreements, taking forward cover, and so on, are an important part of a business. But it is your CFO and CRO, not you, who should have a vision for how their part of the company is going to work seamlessly and effectively for your staff, customers and business partners.

When I hired my first tech engineer at Com Tech, my vision was that if a customer called for support, we would answer calls promptly, and provide accurate information. If we didn't have a response immediately, we would never keep the customer in the dark. How we did that was up to Nathan and Darron (our tech management team). What systems and resources they needed was also up to them – I couldn't give them the authority without the responsibility.

Hands-on attitude

You don't deserve respect, you earn it. You earn it by rolling up your sleeves and working WITH your team, not by having a team work FOR you. We always wanted managers who worked for their team, not the other way around. Of course, you also need to lead: it's your actions – rather than a title on a business card – that will earn you respect.

HR skills

As a founder, you need managers who hire the right people, in terms of both attitude and ability. They need to fire the 'wrong' people as quickly as possible and, importantly, they need to motivate a team of people to be the best that they can possibly be.

This happens in small companies, in sporting teams and in large companies. How often have you seen a soccer team change managers and the very next week that team goes from losing to winning? They have exactly the same players on the field as the previous week – the difference is they now have a manager who knows how to get the best out of a team of people. It happened at Microsoft, which has become one of the most valuable companies in the world, not by bringing in new people or products, but simply by an exceptional empathetic leader galvanising a team *to be the best that they could possibly be.*

— — —

So, on the subject of managers – including you, the founder – I have a few remaining words of advice.

- I have beaten this one to death, but I want to reiterate: surround yourself with highly capable people in those roles that you will never be able to do yourself, or that you may be able to do but don't want to. I remember meeting an older founder who told me that he had finally realised he couldn't do it all on his own. To which I replied, 'That's a strength, not a weakness. Nobody can do everything well.' You're generally either a striker or a defender, a batter or a bowler, a sales specialist or a tech specialist, but rarely both.

- Strive for perfection, but don't let it stop you from executing on your vision. As long as you're not going to let your customers or staff down, don't wait for that perfect product or service – if you do, you may never get to release your product. I couldn't put this any better than Reid Hoffman, founder of LinkedIn: 'If you're not embarrassed by the first version of your product, you've launched too late.' You have to get your product out there to know whether it is solving the problem it was designed for. Once in market you will receive valuable feedback from customers, and this input, together with your own roadmap, will only help you to enhance your solution.

- It's nice to be important, but it's important to be nice. Muhammad Ali famously said that he would like to be remembered 'as a man who never looked down on those who looked up to him.' As a founder you should be humble and expect the same from the management team that you surround yourself with. At the end of the day, we all put our pants on one leg at a time. If anyone watched the memorial tribute to Shane Warne, what was most evident about Warney was not just his amazing feats on the cricket ground, but also the manner in which he treated everyone – no matter their status or wealth. If Warney could be humble, there is no reason for anyone else not to be. We love Ash Barty for the same reason – humble beats arrogant every day.

● ● ●

CHAPTER 21

You gotta know when you gotta go

I always remember sitting in a meeting where we were lucky enough to have legendary Australian cricket captain Ian Chappell (who became a board member of Com Tech) speak to us about leadership.

One of our managers asked Ian, 'How do you know when you have reached your use-by date?' I remember Ian's reply so clearly. He said that when he didn't feel mentally tough enough to lead an Australian cricket team on a gruelling tour of the West Indies, he stepped aside as captain, enabling his brother, Greg, to take his place. A few years later, Ian was asked by Kerry Packer to become captain of an Australian cricket team that was to spearhead World Series Cricket. Kerry knew what an amazing leader of men Ian was.

By 2001, I was totally burnt out – in fact, I was burnt to a cinder. We had grown from 240 people in 1996 to

1400 people by 2000. We had built the largest and most respected network integration company in Australia, but it had taken its toll. I'm not good at much, but I was good with people – staff, customers and business partners. This was the value that I added to the company. My competitive advantage was that I knew everyone in the company, from reception through to sales and tech support. I knew their names and sometimes their partner's and even their kids' names. I knew what their hobbies were, what their challenges were and what their objectives were.

In August 2000, we moved to amazing new premises in a heritage building in Sydney's CBD. I hated it. In our previous, very basic, offices I sat at an open-plan desk right at the front door and saw everyone coming and going. I would ask what deals we were working on, what deals we had won, what I could do to help and what their plans were for the weekend. You could feel the pulse of the company from where I sat. In our new office, they put our GM, CFO, EA, head of M&A and me behind a screen, on a level that was located a long way from the sales team. It was like working in a big corporate. I didn't feel part of the action, I couldn't feel the buzz – and it just wasn't for me anymore.

It was time to say goodbye to my fourth kid. I loved the people and the culture, but I believed that I had lost the ability to make a difference. Everybody should want to add value in a company, no matter their position. Like Ian Chappell, I just felt that I was not mentally tough enough to take the company to the next level. To compound the issue, the CEO of our new owner (Dimension Data) and I each had a different vision for the company's direction. I wanted to invest in the future while our core business was strong and move the company into the internet age – but the global CEO was fixated on the past. I simply didn't have the energy to challenge our new owner. In addition, the dot-com bubble had burst. For the first time in our history, we were laying off staff. It was horrible, it was hard – but necessary for us to stay in business.

When UK television presenter Michael Parkinson interviewed Shane Warne, he asked him why he was retiring from cricket. Warne answered, 'My mentor, Ian Chappell, told me, "Shane, better people ask you why you did than why you didn't."' That was exactly how I felt. In October 2001, I officially walked out of DiData's offices and never walked back in. I still miss the incredible people and can-do culture that we had in Com Tech. I'm proud of what we achieved during my tenure as CEO, but I knew that my time had come.

The two leaders who took over from me – Steve Nola, who ran the integration business, and Ross Cochrane, who took over as CEO of the distribution and training businesses – did a better job than I would have done taking the company to the next level. There's a time for coming and a time for going. I am proud that I hired Steve in 1989 to run our Melbourne office, when he was a young kid of 23. I gave him a sales target of $1.8 million dollars for his first year. We were pretty much doing this without an office, so I wanted to give him a target that he would achieve. I remember Steve's olive skin becoming a pasty white – he nearly fainted. Who would have thought that Steve would go on to run DiData in Australia and preside over a business with more than 2000 people and revenues exceeding a billion dollars? He also ran DiData's global cloud business. This is what makes me feel so proud. So many of us, myself included, achieved so much more than we had ever believed we were capable of. There are other stories similar to Steve's, but to tell them I would have to write another book.

A good leader should be able to motivate a team to be the best they can possibly be. I know that at the outset, many of us at Com Tech (again, I include myself) did not realise that with the right attitude, opportunity and company culture, *anything is possible.*

● ● ●

I believed that I had lost the ability to make a difference. Everybody should want to add value in a company, no matter their position.

CHAPTER 22

From startup to wind down

Have you ever gone from a million miles an hour to zero, in a matter of minutes?

That's what happened to me and it wasn't fun. Going from being totally consumed by my work, to having nothing to do, was debilitating – I was pretty close to depression. I can understand why some elite athletes sink into a deep depression after retiring. It had been essential for me to make a change: I was really burnt out and I badly needed a break. But I hadn't realised that the impact of leaving the company I had founded would be so severe.

The DiData guys had asked me to stay on as non-executive chairman, but I couldn't – I would have found it impossible to be 'half-pregnant' after being so hands-on as a founding CEO. It would not have been fair on the new CEOs for me to be around, potentially undermining their authority. I know that I am not the type of person who would have been able to tell someone who had worked with me for a long period of time, 'Sorry, mate, that's not my job. You need to speak to Steve, Ross or my brother Jon.'

I had been sitting on the board of Fairfax for about two years prior to leaving DiData – and I hated every minute of that experience. Although I worked with some amazing people, sitting on the board of a large public company was not for me. I had committed to three years – and the day that came up, I tendered my resignation. Dave Gonski, one of Australia's finest, asked me to stay, but I told him that if I got hit by a bus the share price of Fairfax wouldn't go up one cent, nor would it go down one cent – because I added absolutely no value. My strength is building teams and creating a can-do culture in smaller companies, not reading reams of documents in a monthly board pack. I didn't feel that I could influence outcomes sitting around a board table. I'm not suggesting that others can't, but for me personally it just didn't work. It was a great lesson to me that life after Com Tech/DiData wouldn't involve sitting on six large company boards.

There are so many books and podcasts on happiness available out there, but it was my uncle Shollie – a special man – who gave me some very sage advice. He said that if you want to be happy in your life, you simply need:

- someone to love
- something to do
- something to look forward to.

I needed something to do!

A year after I left Com Tech, I became executive chairman of a small company called Holly, assisting the CEO, Lance Berks. After six months, Lance said, 'I can't thank you enough for helping me,' and I replied, 'Lance, I can't thank you enough for helping me.' This was my purpose. Once again, I was able to make a difference, only this time I wasn't the main guy – that was Lance. At Com Tech, if I had toothache on Monday I would go to the dentist on Saturday. I naively believed that people would think I had lost my commitment if I was seen leaving work early. It was stupid. Nobody would have cared. At Holly, I could make a difference without being the CEO, and I loved it. This was my future. I loved mentoring founders – sometimes with some equity and often just because I loved making a difference and working with people I wanted to work with.

That's what I have done since 2002. I've worked in many diverse industries, including software for the fast-food industry, a marketplace for fast-moving consumer goods, small-business loans, online insurance, online car sales, augmented reality, cyber security, construction technology, HR tech and even an online diamond exchange – boy, do I wish I hadn't done that one.

When investing, first and foremost I always evaluate the founder. Then I look at the problem they are solving. Lastly, I assess how big an opportunity it represents. The founder has the domain expertise, and hopefully I can add value through my experience of building a fast-growing company. Finally, age has its benefits.

Prior to setting up a VC fund, where my business partners and I manage other people's money, I didn't even care about the opportunity or market potential – I only cared about wanting to add value to a founder. Any return would have simply been a bonus.

I've failed twice when I backed the wrong founder, even though I knew I should never have invested in the first place. I've also failed when I didn't back the *right* founder, just because I didn't like the valuation. My biggest failure was not backing Nick Molnar, founder of Afterpay. We had just invested in Zip Money at a $2 million valuation. Nick was raising $6 million at a $20 million pre-money valuation. I told him that if he had the cash at that valuation he should grab it – and if he didn't, then come back and see me. To make things worse, I told Nick (who I've known since he was a kid) that he reminded me of a young David Shein – who I obviously didn't think much of, because

I didn't back him. Afterpay has since been acquired by US-based Square for $39 billion – boy that hurts! It was an expensive lesson: always pay a premium for an exceptional founder. If there is any consolation, at the time of writing this book Zip was worth about $5 billion (my first unicorn as a venture capitalist) and the return was better than it would have been had I invested in Afterpay. As my dad taught me, your profit is made in the buying, not in the selling. However, I could have and should have done both.

Having dabbled in startups for 15 years, along with my business partner Geoff Levy, it was time to formalise things. Together with Jerry Stesel and Laurence Schwartz, we set up a venture capital fund: OIF VC. OIF has been built on what we refer to as the three 'F's.

FOUNDERS We know how tough it is to be a founder and we will do whatever it takes to help our founders realise their dreams, in addition to just writing a cheque. We sincerely regard our founders as our customers.

FUND Our other customers are our investors, who have entrusted us to manage their money, and we owe it to them to get a great return on their investment. However, we would rather make a 5x return with a happy founder than make 7x and say, 'boy, did we screw the founder!'

FUN We're a *fund* without a *d*. We invest in founders that we want to partner with. Our formula is simple – back exceptional founders who are easy to work with. Life's too short to work with people who aren't aligned with your cultural values.

I hope that I can continue to add value to my partners, to our investors and, importantly, to our fearless founders, for many more years to come.

● ● ●

If you want to be happy in your life, you simply need:

- someone to love
- something to do
- something to look forward to.

CHAPTER 23

Regrets, I've had a few

When I turned 60 in October 2020, it gave me time to reflect on my life and career.

What did I do well, what could I have done better and what advice would I give to my younger self?

I was a young founder: 26 when I started, 40 when I sold and 41 when I left the company that I had founded. Yes, I was burnt out and needed a breather, but throwing in the towel so early has definitely been a regret. At risk of sounding arrogant, I know that, together with an unbelievable team, I was a good founder who had both vision and people skills. I think that I had at least another startup in me, but at the time I thought I was done.

When I see the amazing success that Australia is achieving, I wish I was part of this phenomenal era for innovation in this country. My original business, Com Tech, was built riding on the coat-tails of successful companies like Microsoft and Cisco – selling industry-standard, market-leading, generally American products in Australia. My dream was to do it the other way round: build a market-leading product in Australia and then lead the world. I'm so proud of what Scott and Mike of Atlassian and Mel and Cliff of Canva have achieved – they have paved the way for others, the fruits of which we are already witnessing.

Australia is on the map as a global powerhouse for innovation, and boy do I wish that was me. So to all the young founders out there: don't quit once you have achieved financial success – it's only a small part, albeit an important part, of your life journey.

I never dreamed of the financial success that I would achieve, and I probably ended up having a small-business mentality. I got rid of my winners too early, and lived by the adage 'nobody ever went broke selling at a profit' – always happy with making a profit as opposed to thinking, *how big could this opportunity really be?* I always felt that I fluked it once in my life and that my job was to hold on to my cash – rather than thinking, *that was easy* and believing I could easily do it again. When I invested in Zip at a $2 million valuation, I never envisaged that the company would be worth more than $20 million. So, when it got to $200 million,

I couldn't believe my luck. Instead of looking at how well Larry and Pete were executing and how they were capitalising on the industry change from credit to debit cards, I was happy to cash in on my winner. It was way too early! I could have sold Zip at a market valuation of $5 billion, although since the world's economy has changed, it's back at about $500 million. Knowing when to sell is key.

Back in 2020, one of our outstanding founders called and said, 'Dave, based on a $600 million offer, we have the opportunity that could deliver $50 million to each of the founders – it's life changing, but we think we can build a $10 billion business. What should we do?' Lucky they called me at 60 and not when I was still a young 59-year-old, as I would probably have given them a different answer. Instead, my response was: 'Guys, if you genuinely believe that this is a $10 billion business, don't get rid of your company too early – it may never happen again. Perhaps you can each take a few million off the table now, pay for a home for your family and then continue along the journey.' I know that was good advice, as they have just taken on new capital at a $1.2 billion valuation. Imagine what Mark Zuckerburg would have left on the table if he had taken the $15 billion deal offered by Microsoft in 2007. A gutsy call – but obviously Zuck had the conviction that this was only the beginning.

Following on from this, I wish I hadn't sold all of Com Tech to Dimension Data. If I had my way again, I would have kept our distribution business, a part of the company non-strategic to our new owners. While no business is easy, it was definitely the easiest of our three business units – systems integration, technical training and distribution – to manage. We simply had to deliver the right products on time to our customers around Australia. The distribution business was dependent on great systems and good people. And it scaled well: because of the systems, you didn't need to keep hiring people as the revenue grew. In 2014, the distribution business was sold to Dicker Data, who at the time had a market valuation of $133 million; today Dicker Data is valued at $1.6 billion. A large part of that growth in valuation would have come from our distribution business – clearly one of the deals of the decade.

With that off my chest, I'm still proud to be a small part of the ecosystem and to have had the privilege of working with some amazing founders: young, old, male, female, from big cities and small towns. I hope that one day people will be talking about our founders like they speak of Larry and Peter from Zip, Nick and Anthony from Afterpay, Richard White from WiseTech Global – and, of course, Scott and Mike, who led the way.

● ● ●

To all the young founders out there: don't quit once you have achieved financial success – it's only a small part, albeit an important part, of your life journey. But you still need to wake up with a purpose every day.

CHAPTER 24

Tips for founders

First and foremost, let me say that the most important ingredient for a successful startup is the founder.

In fact, at OIF we judge each opportunity on what we refer to as the '5 Ts' when considering whether to invest or not. These 'Ts' are:

1. **Team** – If we don't love the team, we don't care about points 2–5 below.

2. **TAM** – What is the total addressable market of the problem the product solves?

3. **Traction** – How much business has the company generated and are the customers referenceable?

4. **Timing** – Is it too early OR has the opportunity passed? (An amazing founder like Nick Molnar at Afterpay had the timing right. Had he started a few years later – same founder, same thesis – the ship would already have sailed.)

5. **Terms** – Is the deal fair for both the founder and our fund?

VC companies invariably back the jockey, not just the idea. Remember, nobody knows a business and its potential as well as the founder. If you can't deliver with confidence and passion, nobody will be able to sell your idea.

- **Leave the advisor at the door**

   If you can't pitch your business yourself, how will you attract staff, customers and business partners to your company? After all, VCs are investing in the founder.

- **Clearly articulate the problem you are solving and how your product solves that problem**

   Keep the message simple – don't be tempted to overcomplicate it. Keeping your points simple and clear is always best. Remember, simplicity is the ultimate sophistication.

- **How big is the opportunity?**

   What is the total addressable market?

- **What traction have you achieved to date?**

   If you already have customers, it's important that these customers would be more than happy to act as a reference for both the product and the manner in which your company has conducted itself. There is no better salesperson than a happy customer. A great customer reference is the best validation that your product does indeed solve a problem.

- **What is your business model and, importantly, what are the unit economics?**

  At some stage every company needs to make a profit. It's really important to demonstrate that your unit economics for the sale of a product can generate a profit; i.e., your revenue is greater than the cost of whatever you are selling. Never has this become more important, and chapter 6 explains the challenges.

- **How much do you need?**

  How will the funds that you are raising be used to help you take your business to the next stage?

- **Leave the valuation to the experts**

  If you don't like the valuation that you are offered, go elsewhere. If all VCs' valuations are within the same ballpark, don't just take the highest offer. Choose the partner with whom you feel most culturally aligned and who genuinely wants to add value to your business. Make sure that you call as many of the founders in their portfolio as possible to ensure that their words match their actions.

The pitch deck

One of the most important functions of a founder is the ability to raise capital. As a partner in a VC fund, I have had the privilege of reviewing many pitch decks – we see about 20 opportunities per week. You need to produce a deck that will quickly capture attention. I thought I would share one of the best I have come across – I liked it because it was simple, with the founder being able to explain everything a VC would

Slide 1: Snapshot

What problem are you solving?:

Your solution:

Your business model:

The team:

Traction to date:

Go to market (GTM):

Your revenue forecast:

Your ask:

ask in a single page. The detail followed in later slides, but I got the gist in 30 seconds – a great example of an 'elevator pitch'. I have taken the liberty of sharing this pitch deck below. (Okay, there are two slides, the second showing the growth opportunities of the solution if Slide 1 captures your potential investor's attention.) I hope you find this as useful as I did when I was pitched by the founder.

Slide 2: Growth Plan

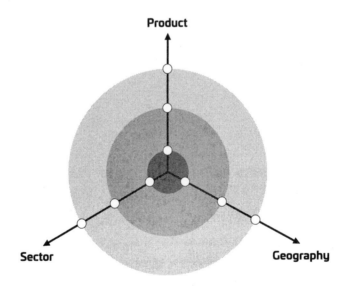

Below are six emails that I sent to OIF VC's founders: two at the start of the COVID-19 pandemic, one a year later, two in 2022 and one in 2023.

Leading during tough times

17 March 2020

Guys

I hope that you and your families are managing during these unprecedented times. Who would have thought???

I will never forget catching up with Steve Vamos (now CEO of Xero) when he was CEO of Apple Australia. Apple in those days was about to go broke – yep, they nearly went bust. I asked Steve how things were going and he looked at me and said, 'Dave, for the last two years I have had to make shit taste like chocolate.' That to me was the sign of a great leader. It's easy to be positive when things are going well – how you lead when the shit hits the fan will mean the difference between a company that makes things happen vs a company that says: what happened? If you look dejected, your team will be dejected. They are looking to you for guidance and support. This is your time to lead. We are ALL in uncharted waters, but one of the few benefits of being nearly 60 is that you have experience on your side. While all triggered by different events, I have seen the 1987 stock market crash, I have seen the dot-com crash, I was there for the GFC and together we now all witness and have to navigate a global pandemic.

I know that many of you may have read the Sequoia Capital note which Jerry posted on Slack, so I won't bore you with the same information.

I wanted to share an update from the company Auckland Airport (attached to this email), where you will see that a company worth $1.2 billion today, which was only a few weeks ago valued at $2.4 billion, has cancelled their dividend and announced a wide range of cost-cutting measures including:

1. Hiring freeze

2. A suspension of all discretionary spending

3. A review of work underway with external consultants

4. In addition, the CEO has volunteered to cut his salary by 20 per cent and the board will cut their fees too

Guys, you have bust your butts to get your companies to where they are today. Like the CEO of Auckland Airport, nobody anticipated that planes would not be flying, that restaurants and cafes would be closing and, tragically, people will be dying as a result of an illness that none of us had heard of only a few months ago.

I started my company in 1987. It was at the height of the stock market crash. By keeping my costs down I gave myself the best shot of surviving and thriving. Com Tech went on to become the largest networking company in Australia – started during the toughest year since the Great Depression. My competitors were not as frugal as me and many went out of business while Com Tech grew market share. I saw this again during the dot-com crash in 2000. Some of the world's greatest companies were built during that era – Amazon, Google and eBay – but many did not survive. Unlike many of the companies that failed during the dot-com era, your companies are advanced enough to show that you truly solve customers' problems. You all have amazing products and you have revenue. You now need to manage your business for the market today, not yesterday – it's different. You may have to make some hard decisions, but once again, only from experience, make the tough ones early.

Your friend in these times is CASH. You have to do whatever it takes to reduce your burn, reduce your churn and EXTEND YOUR RUNWAY. Auckland Airport will not be the only company that implements cost-cutting measures which may mean a suspension of discretionary spending – your sales WILL be impacted. The companies that survive these challenges will come out better and stronger and could be the next Atlassian – the future is in your hands, with all the help and support that you need from OIF. You know that you can call 24 x 7 – that's what we are here for!!

Best Rgds

Team OIF

— — —

26 March 2020

Good Morning or Good Evening to those in the US

I just wanted to drop you all a quick note to see how you, your families and teams are managing during these extraordinary times.

It has amazed me how resilient you, our founders, have been during this time. Going from growth founders to survival founders in a matter of weeks is something that one can't learn at Harvard Business School. Your leadership skills have been put to the test. I want to thank each and every one of you for the commitment that you have made. I know many of you have made personal financial sacrifices in terms of salary reductions to reduce your burn – your wealth will ultimately be from the equity of your startup that you have created.

More difficult has been putting off outstanding people – this takes a massive psychological toll. I always say it's easy to hire people, very hard to get rid of people. Working from home (WFH), when a core part of your company's advantage has been the team culture that you have created in your workplace, has its challenges too. When this is all over, and it will be, when someone says let's WFH, I think the answer will be WTF. Working from home in itself can be challenging – working in isolation when everyone thrives in a group environment, dealing with kids, as well as the worry of 'will someone near and dear to me be infected by this virus?'

I was lucky enough to have Bob Mansfield (who I have copied on this email) as my chairman during some of the toughest times during my time as founder of Com Tech. Bob was formerly CEO of McDonald's and founding CEO of Optus. Just having someone to bounce ideas, fears and unknowns off made a big difference to me. If you have someone like that, USE that person – they may not have all the answers, but just knowing there is someone around is so important. It is critical at a time like this that you, as a leader of people, feel strong enough to work through this crisis.

Once again, if Jerry, Laurence, Isabella, Geoff or me can be of any assistance through this time, please know that you can contact any of us at anytime.

Best Rgds, thank you and importantly stay well

David

— — —

26 March 2021

Hi Guys

A year ago (17 March 2020), as we stared down the rapidly evolving and unknown COVID-19 crisis, I wrote an email to you titled *Leading during tough times.*

While we couldn't anticipate, or far less imagine, just how tough the times would be, we suggested you should do whatever it took to extend your cash runway and manage your business for the market today, not yesterday – it would be fundamentally different.

The unprecedented times meant significant uncertainty. What became apparent was that many of us, if not all of us, would be faced with hard decisions, and experience had taught us that tough decisions needed early and decisive action.

While we are not out of the woods and challenges will continue, let me tell you that what hasn't changed is that we are incredibly proud of the resilience you and your teams have shown. I hope you take a moment to reflect, be proud of your efforts and continue to keep the wellbeing of your team at the core of what you do moving forward – a dream with no team is just an idea.

Reflecting on where we are today, I am confident that there has never been a better time to be investing in the future. Your business models coupled with your own determination have demonstrated the impact of the problems you solve. But now may be the time to put your foot on the gas.

Today, a year after our *Leading during tough times* email, I urge you 'not to be reckless in either direction'. By that I mean, make sure that you do whatever it takes to give you and your team the best possible opportunity to maximise the potential of your company.

We challenge you to be bold, be critical, think beyond what's achievable tomorrow and ask yourselves:

- Do you have enough cash to take advantage of the opportunity ahead?

- What key positions do you need to fill to build the most effective team to get to where you need to be?

- Are you ready to open offices in different geographies once travel opens up?

- What gaps do you need to fill in your product to put daylight between you and your competitors – how are you building a bigger moat?

I thought that I would like to share a note from Sequoia Capital, headlined: *Accelerate plans amid signs of recovery.*

Like OIF, last year Sequoia Capital sent a note to all their founders warning of an impending storm. On 19 March 2021, a year later, Sequoia sent a note advising their founders to accelerate plans amid signs of recovery. Leonardo da Vinci said, 'good artists copy, great artists steal', so below are some of the points from the Sequoia letter to their founders, together with a bit of poetic licence (*in italics*).

I have included the link to their full note below, and I quote:

While the pandemic is far from over, we see an important window of opportunity opening up right now. The US *(where many of you now gain a large chunk of your revenue)* is poised for stronger economic growth in the second half of 2021 than we've seen in decades. If you feel confident about your business, now is the time to start carefully putting your foot on the accelerator. In many ways, COVID pulled forward the future that technology companies have been building.

Our advice for founders and CEOs

No one can say for certain what the future holds. Remain deliberate and measured (*don't be reckless in either direction*), but don't be afraid to dream and be optimistic about where the world is going. This will enable you to focus on your long-term aspirations while navigating the next few quarters, no matter what they bring.

Reassess/reaffirm your why: As you prepare to accelerate, reassess or reaffirm your long-term mission. Then, challenge yourself and your team: are you dreaming big enough?

Remain measured: You've made really hard decisions during the pandemic, but you realised how nimble and efficient your company became. You found more cost-effective ways to reach customers when you reset marketing spend. Don't lose your hard-earned operating rhythm, even if you believe the future is bright (*you can't afford to be reckless in either direction*).

Prepare for more volatility: While you prepare to take advantage of the opportunities ahead, remain nimble as you fine tune your tactics. Knowing when to upshift and downshift in changing conditions will be important moving forward *(you can't afford to be reckless in either direction).*

Focus on what matters: Don't get distracted by vanity metrics. Stimulus spending and monetary policy have helped create buoyancy in public and private markets and some of you may find you can fundraise at attractive valuations. If so, take advantage of your good fortunes *(provided there is a good cultural fit with the investor).* Enduring companies focus on the things that matter and build value for their customers, employees, *business partners,* communities and shareholders.

Most importantly, focus on the wellbeing of your number one asset, your people: Remote work has proven many benefits. However, for many the line between work and personal life has dissolved and it's taking its toll on mental health. Employees are burning out and feeling isolated after a year at home. Strong leadership that puts people first will continue to be critical. The last year has been trying in ways we couldn't have imagined. It's been exhausting. However, change also brings opportunity. At Sequoia *(and OIF),* we believe anything is possible. Your resilience, creativity and ability to rapidly pivot throughout the pandemic is proof.

Here is a link to the full note:

www.dealstreetasia.com/stories/sequoia-letter-232633/

A final word about great leadership. We are indeed extremely lucky and privileged to live in Australia, and the manner in which our leaders, national and state, have handled the pandemic has been world class, but I did want to single one leader out. To be a leader you need the energy to deal with not only the knowns but as importantly the unknowns. Consider that over the last year, there has been drought, bushfires, pandemic and now floods. That wasn't in the NSW Government's business plan.

I wanted to wish everyone in your team as well as your families a rejuvenating, safe and happy time over Easter, Passover and school holidays. May you enjoy the time doing the things you love with those you love.

Thank you for your phenomenal support and enjoy the weekend

Team OIF – Jerry, Laurence, Isabella, Geoff, Paul, Emily, Ryan and David

— — —

5 February 2022

Hi Guys

I hope that you and your families all had an awesome break and managed to recharge for the year ahead. Hopefully Omicron didn't impact your plans too much, although so hard to avoid!!

I was originally going to write a note about the state of the stock market, but after reading Paul Bassat's (Square Peg and SEEK founder) comments I decided that I would leave that to him – see *AFR* articles below

www.afr.com/chanticleer/tech-valuations-are-dropping-but-vc-leaders-are-unfazed-20220124-p59quq

www.afr.com/technology/it-s-a-stock-pickers-market-top-tech-investors-see-long-term-buys-20220127-p59rni

In a nutshell, what is happening in the public markets eventually HAS TO FLOW down into the private markets. It doesn't mean that any of the companies that have been impacted are bad companies – they have just been revalued. The average decline from the 52-week high for the NASDAQ index constituents is 48%, and 10% have declined by more than 70%. While not quite dot-com era declines, the reality is that true growth companies have experienced a substantial decline in their valuations in recent months. So, if I had written the article, my key point would have been that if you are going to need to raise capital, DO IT NOW before it becomes harder to raise at the valuations that you are seeking to achieve. Like

Spotify, Shopify, Square, Monday, Hubspot, you have great companies with amazing opportunities. BUT valuations may change, so if you need to raise, now is the time. However, I do think the good times (see the article on Dovetail below) may be over – well, at least for now.

www.afr.com/technology/dovetail-confirms-960m-valuation-in-bubble-like-environment-20220118-p59p4x?btis

If you are a good founder (and you must be if OIF VC invested in your company ☺) and you have been executing since your last raise, raising capital is easy. The valuations may change over time, but there is so much capital in the venture space today, you should be able to get that raise away.

So I wanted to bring up what I believe is the biggest challenge facing a founder today. People. Attracting, engaging and retaining people has never been tougher, and for you to continue to build world-class organisations your focus should be on ensuring that you don't just leave this task to your People and Culture or Chief Happiness Officer. As you may have witnessed first-hand, it's pretty self-evident what is happening in the market today (if you haven't, see the article below.)

War for talent: 'People have gone from $150,000 to $250,000 per year'
www.afr.com/leadership/careers/rise-of-the-counter-offer-tech-workers-offered-up-to-100-000-to-stay-20220201-p59sxn?btis

As a founder, motivating your team is a critical part of your job description – you are the competitive advantage. You have to be investing a big chunk of your time to ensure that you continue to recruit the best – and that once on board, they want to stay with your company. It doesn't just happen, it requires a big investment, and I'm not just referring to salary and options – I'm talking about time!

Have a great weekend and, as always, if we can be of any support, please don't hesitate to give us a shout – anytime!

Best Rgds

David and Team OIF VC

— — —

25 May 2022

Hi Guys,

I hope that you and your families are all doing well.

I had to look at the note below that I sent to you, our founders, more than two years ago. To be frank, I have been surprised by what has occurred since the start of the pandemic – I didn't expect the growth rates and level of investment that occurred following the massive pullback in March 2020. Nor did I expect that my message then, would be way more applicable today, considering what has transpired in the public markets over the past few months.

I don't think that I could articulate any better than what is outlined by A16Z, Y combinator and Fred Wilson links below. I highly recommend that you read all articles.

What I will add is that I will never forget that at my graduation ceremony in 1985, the person delivering the speech said – 'In my lifetime, there have been eight recessions and seven booms, so I guess we're heading for another boom.' So, the good news is that while the good times had to eventually come to an end, so will the tough times – it's just a matter of how long they will last and how deep they will be. The key is for you, as leaders, to navigate through the tough times that we will all inevitably be exposed to over the next period. You can only control what is in your control – runway, unit economics, customer and staff satisfaction. Remember, if you get this right, you will emerge at the other side with more market share, less competition and a better business than what you have today.

As always, the team at OIF VC are here to support you and your teams. If you need input regarding how best to optimise your runway (based on formula provided by A16Z) please don't hesitate to contact Jerry, Laurence, Isabella, Anna or Ollie.

https://future.a16z.com/framework-valuation-navigating-down-markets/?utm_campaign=future&utm_medium=social&utm_source=linkedin

https://techcrunch-com.cdn.ampproject.org/c/s/techcrunch.com/2022/05/19/yc-advises-founders-to-plan-for-the-worst/amp/

https://avc.com/2022/05/how-this-ends-2/

Best Rgds,

David and Team OIF VC

— — —

21 April 2023

Hi Guys,

I wanted to make you an offer that you can't refuse.

I'm offering anyone the opportunity to get a 100% refund on their movie ticket if what I commit to below is not fulfilled, and yes, if you buy popcorn, I will pay for that too!!

You have to take your partner, your co-founder, your sales team to watch the movie *Air*.

As founders, we are always selling – selling to staff, selling to customers, selling to business partners and selling to VCs (we're selling to founders).

Here, in no particular order, are some takeaways that you can expect to learn:

1. The power of persistence

2. The importance of teamwork – no deal is ever won by a single person

3. The importance of innovation

4. Taking a risk that could prove to be a company-changing opportunity

5. Doing your homework to know what your competition will be doing and how to sell on your strengths against a massive incumbent

6. Identifying the real decision maker

7. How the founder needs to support their team

8. Courage to do things that are way out of the ordinary

9. Authenticity generally wins

10. The importance of taking two hours of your day to unwind and enjoy a movie

If I have let you down, send me your bank account details and I will personally pay for the tickets, popcorn and Slurpee.

Importantly, take time on ANZAC Day to never forget the courage and sacrifice of the ANZAC soldiers who have served and died in service of our great country – Lest We Forget.

Have an awesome weekend.

David, Geoff, Jerry, Laurence, Issy, Ollie, Andrew, Adam, Dave, Kevin and Keren

— — —

Acknowledgments

In writing this book I've mentioned just a few of the people who made Com Tech and later Dimension Data the amazing company that it was. There are literally way too many to have named all the sensational people who helped me navigate the ups and downs during my 14 years as founder of Com Tech. I want to acknowledge all of the people who worked with me from those early years until I stepped down in 2001 – I could never have achieved what I did without you. I always say that 99 per cent of the good ideas at Com Tech came from people other than me – so thank you for your contribution to building Australia's first tech unicorn. I hope that our success helped to inspire other founders.

Please note that where possible I have endeavoured to attribute all the quotations that appear in these pages. I have always been fascinated by business leadership, and over the years I have read and listened to much; if I have failed to mention the source, apologies, but you have inspired me and I hope that my words, influenced by yours, will inspire many others. I would be pleased to receive information about any material that requires further acknowledgment in subsequent printings of this book.